VIDA

vida

Empowering
Residents

Transforming
Communities

Ron Lovett

LIONCREST
PUBLISHING

VIDA

Empowering Residents, Transforming Communities

FIRST EDITION

ISBN   978-1-5445-4753-4   *Hardcover*
       978-1-5445-4752-7   *Paperback*
       978-1-5445-4754-1   *Ebook*

Contents

Foreword

THERE'S A RIDE AT DISNEY WORLD CALLED IT'S A SMALL World. You step into a small wooden boat and float gently down a sparkling lazy river. Soft, bouncy music plays in the background as you drift past magical creatures tucked among the trees. The air smells like a lush, living forest—every sense invited into a calm, enchanted adventure.

That's what I thought it would be like after Ron sold his security company—a fixed ride like It's a Small World, even if for a short period of time. Of course, it was nothing like that. It was much more like stepping onto the Scrambler and holding on for dear life.

While we did initially take a few weeks to travel, three weeks after Ron sold his security company, I found myself on our first vacation, pregnant, with a toddler on my hip, talking about how no one has ever truly reinvented the toilet. I knew where that conversation was going.

I was deep enough into my marriage to know that if my husband had a thought, that thought would turn into chicken scratches on a napkin, which would then turn into 65 phone calls with people who could start executing on the "next big idea." That was the challenge with Ron: while he was amazing at dreaming, he was even better at execution, and that's a scary combination for someone who really just wants to sit in the magical forest for a minute to smell the roses.

While he wrestled with a couple of different industries that spoke to him, real estate was a steady drum in the background. Ron bought his first property at 20 years old and intuitively added another handful of residential properties, followed by a couple of multifamily properties, over the next decade. He acquired these properties almost as unconsciously as I brushed my teeth in the morning, which, looking back, should have been telling in regard to what his next entrepreneurial chapter would be.

But there was a missing link to innovation in the affordable housing space. That piece didn't fully click until one of Ron's roughest buildings turned into a scene from *Bad Boys*. Cleaning up the physical space was one thing, but managing the people inside, some of whom were putting single moms and hardworking families at risk, was just as tough.

That's when Ron first dropped the line that started it all: "What if I revolutionized the affordable housing industry?"

In 2018, it wasn't a crisis. It was ignored. Affordable housing was the forgotten child of real estate—too often left in the hands of landlords who reinforced every negative stereotype.

Slumlord came to mind after I did a bit of on-the-ground recon with Ron. I remember thinking:

How is he going to tackle this? It's just too big!

People walked around the buildings with no shoes. The units were a disaster. If you brought a good, solid butter knife, you could open any front door or unit you desired. To say I didn't immediately see the appeal would be an understatement.

But Ron could see past all of that. And here's the thing: I'd seen him do it before. I watched him take an outdated, dysfunctional private security industry and transform it through innovation and a decentralization model. This wasn't new territory. And once he locked on to a challenge, there was no turning back.

He got to work on the model, mapping out the patterns to understand what made these forgotten properties fail and imagining how they could become places of pride again.

The cracks in the system weren't random. Everything kept pointing back to four recurring pain points in workforce housing: lack of ownership, safety, belonging, and community. If Ron could solve for those, if he could spark pride and purpose and tap into the skills people already had, he could shake this industry up in a way no one ever had.

This wasn't just about one building or one city. He was starting to see the shape of a model that could work—not only in Halifax, Nova Scotia, but across Canada and beyond. Something that could have a real, lasting impact on a global scale.

It was big enough to go all in. He shelved the napkin sketches of reinvented toilets and other fly-by-night ideas. He had found the mountain worth climbing, but this time, he was wearing armour forged from experience, purpose, and the lessons of every business that came before.

This is an entrepreneurial love story for the ages.

XO.

—NATALIE

Introduction

MOST PEOPLE HAVE NO IDEA HOW BROKEN THIS INDUS-try really is.

They hear "housing crisis" and think the solution is just to build more. But what we're facing isn't just a supply problem. It's an affordability crisis. A cost-of-delivery crisis.

Even with free land and no profit, delivering a new unit in cities like Vancouver can still cost over $1 million. And the new builds we keep hearing about? They're already priced too high, and they'll take 30 years to filter down into something remotely affordable, if they ever do.

Meanwhile, the buildings that are affordable—the older ones—are being bought, renovated, and flipped for profit. The very stock that could help solve the problem is being turned into the next crisis.

So no, we can't build our way out. Not fast enough. Not affordably enough. Not for the people who need housing today.

I didn't come from this world. I didn't have a real estate background. But I did have one thing: an instinct for broken systems. I love taking stale industries and flipping them on their head. That's what pushed me to ask the question that changed everything:

What if I revolutionized the affordable housing industry?

Not tweaked it. Not improved it. Flipped it. Rebuilt it from the ground up.

What if we could actually preserve affordability and build something that truly worked for the people living in it? What if housing was the ground floor for pride and dignity, not just shelter?

Now, one might naturally assume we'd go the nonprofit or community housing route. And I get that question all the time: "Why not a nonprofit?"

The issue I had with that route is you can't fix housing at scale, especially if it depends on government grants to function. I've seen too many well-intentioned nonprofits do great work only to get kneecapped by a funding cut or policy shift.

And there was no way I was going to build a business based on whichever way the political wind blew. That's not fair to Canadians, and that's not how you scale anything with staying power.

And not to give anything away here, but five years and 3,000 units later, I can tell you with certainty it would've been categorically impossible to do this work inside that system.

So we built VIDA.

It didn't start big. Just a few small buildings in Halifax. Run-down. Neglected.

We didn't slap on new paint and jack up the rent. We rolled up our sleeves. Talked to the people living there. *Listened*. And then we did something that doesn't happen in this industry: we started working with them.

We didn't see tenants. We saw customers. People who wanted to live in a place they could be proud of. So we treated them that way. We asked what mattered. Safety. Cleanliness. Community. Opportunity. Those became our filters—our four pillars.

And then we did something no one expected: we handed over leadership.

Not to property managers. To the residents themselves. An innovative resident-led housing model never seen before. We empowered them to run their own buildings, called them Building Ambassadors. It was a side hustle, an opportunity to earn extra income and lead where they live. We backed them. Held them accountable.

We developed the Community Contractor program, teaching residents real skills, like how to paint, caulk, and mud. We ran workshops. Trained them through unit turns. This kept customer engagement high and operating costs low.

It started with one building. Then another. Over time, we realized we weren't just acquiring buildings. We were building a platform. Not software, though we've built some, but a real operating system. The structure that holds it all together and makes it scale.

We built systems that balanced autonomy with structure—rhythms and tools to make sure our frontline leaders had what they needed. A sophisticated blend of grassroots and tech. We tracked costs in real time. Turned customer insights into playbooks. Shared data. Shared pride.

This is what true decentralization looks like when it works. When you stop trying to control everything from the top and start trusting the people closest to the problem to lead the solution.

We're not perfect. But we're proving that affordable housing can be preserved without giving up on quality, service, or performance.

This book is the story of how we got to where we are today. What we learned. What broke us open. What made us better. But you'll learn it's about more than housing.

It's a story of reinvention.

Of customers being empowered.

Of an innovative resident-led model built on trust.

And of being stubborn as hell about what matters.

PART 1

What Have
I Gotten
Myself Into?

CHAPTER 1

Innovation Under Pressure

IT'S FUNNY THE THINGS YOU REMEMBER WHEN YOU look back. You'd think, after all we've built, I'd remember the moment I signed the papers, the first time VIDA's name was printed on a lease, or the day we hit 1,000 units. But no. What I remember is the roaches with my first really challenging building.

They were everywhere. In the walls. In the floors. Crawling out of the goddamn electrical outlets. It looked like a lost cause from every angle: inside, outside, and anywhere in between. A relic of neglect standing in Halifax, Nova Scotia. The kind of place people whispered about but avoided at all costs.

I remember the first time I stepped inside. The air was thick and stale, equal parts mould and desperation. The floors, where they weren't buried under debris, were peeling and covered in stains I didn't want to name. The walls had been punched, kicked, and burned. And the roaches didn't even scatter when the lights flicked on. They had won this place long ago.

I stood there, taking it all in, and thought, *What the hell have I gotten myself into?* Cleaning up a place like that isn't a job for the faint of heart. Luckily, I had Cliff.

Cliff was a junk removal guy from North Preston, a tight-knit community just outside Halifax, known for its deep roots and unshakable resilience. He was one of those people who knew everyone and could handle anything. He had this booming, contagious laugh, like life was in on a joke only he could hear. He was fearless. I don't think there was a single thing in that building that rattled him.

One day, after he'd cleaned out what was easily the worst unit I'd ever seen, I found him in the parking lot, leaning against his truck, wiping sweat from his forehead with the bottom of his faded shirt. I told him he'd just pulled off the impossible and thanked him. I had no clue how we would have done it without him.

Cliff grinned and shrugged. "Ah, don't worry about it...but I did get into a little trouble," he said.

I raised an eyebrow. "Yeah? What kind of trouble?"

"Well," he continued, "it was a big job, so I had my wife give me a hand." He paused, shaking his head with a chuckle. "Next day, she told me she's got bites all over her. I told her, 'Don't worry, honey. That was just me giving you nibbles while we were making love.'"

I doubled over laughing. The way Cliff saw the world, even the worst situations had room for a punchline. That's the kind of guy you need on a job like this.

With the building emptied, we moved on to renovations. That's when I learned that cockroaches don't just go away. We sprayed. We fumigated. We ripped out walls. Nothing worked.

I had secured funding from Nova Scotia Housing, taken on debt from the bank, and planned for contingencies. But this? This infestation didn't just eat into the budget; it chewed right through it. Construction projects always have surprises.

But this wasn't a surprise. This was a war. And we were losing.

Or so it seemed.

The thing about inspiration is that you never know when or how it will hit. For me, it happened in the Nashville airport when "Under Pressure" started playing (fittingly, of course). And like some deeply ingrained reflex from years of questionable 1990s DJ mash-ups, my brain immediately jumped to "Ice Ice Baby."

That's when it came to me. I grabbed my phone and googled, *At what temperature do German cockroaches die?*

The answer: they die within a week at 0°C. At –10°C, they die in hours. I checked the weather in Halifax.

The temperature was set to drop to –15°C.

And with that, an unconventional but, dare I say, brilliant plan was born. Sure, slightly crazy, reckless, and probably against some regulation I hadn't thought about. But what did I have to lose?

I called Lekas, my construction lead. "I need you to do something," I said. "Shut off all the water. Pull the sprinkler heads. Lock the doors."

He hesitated. "What are we doing?"

"We're going to freeze the building!"

After a long pause, his eyes opened wide. "You serious?"

"Dead serious. Ice ice baby!"

So that was what we did. We let the building turn into a goddamn icebox.

A week later, we went back inside. The air was sharp, the kind that burns your lungs when you breathe it in. It was silent. Still. I walked through the frozen hallways, waiting for the familiar skittering sound of cockroach legs against linoleum. Nothing.

To be sure, we ran a test. We placed eight Big Macs, cut into quarters, on sticky pads throughout the building.

Not a single Big Mac was touched. The Hail Mary had worked!

And just like that, I was officially in the affordable housing space. Trial by fire—or in this case, ice.

* * *

People call it a housing crisis, but for many, housing has always been a crisis. Others are just now noticing because it's creeping into their world.

Housing costs are going up. Groceries cost more. Wages aren't keeping pace. For renters, it's even tougher. Rents for units built after 2020 can be as much as 200% higher than older buildings. At the same time, Canada will be short 3.5 million homes by 2030, but rising costs, labour shortages, and endless regulatory delays mean we're not building nearly enough to close the gap. The truth is that even if we build more, it won't be enough to solve the problem.

As I write this in 2025, we're watching a shift. Here in Canada, we're moving from a housing crisis to a full-blown affordability crisis. We need a new blueprint that doesn't just focus on building more but also protects the affordable housing we still have.

And let's be real. I wasn't supposed to be the guy to take on housing. I didn't have a background in real estate. I wasn't a developer or a property manager. But what I did have were an instinct for broken systems and the grit to fix them. Maybe that's because of where I came from.

I grew up watching my single mom work relentlessly to keep a roof over our heads. For years, that roof was my grandmother's house. Not because we wanted to live there but because rent anywhere else was out of reach. When my mom remarried, things didn't get easier. My stepfather was verbally abusive and made it painfully clear that I wasn't worth his time, belief, or support. That leaves a mark when you're a kid.

And my biological father? I didn't meet him until I was 21. He shared his regrets and why he hadn't been around. That's a story for another time, but it only fuelled my fire. I'd spent my whole life being underestimated—by my stepfather, my community, and a father who vanished before I could prove him wrong.

That kind of doubt didn't break me. It built my biggest advantage.

When people write you off early, you either let that define you or you learn to bet on yourself. You push through. You keep showing up. You fight for something better, even when the odds say you shouldn't.

That fight started young, way before I knew what I was fighting for. I was scrappy—relentless, curious, always poking at the edges, which of course got me into trouble in the early days. I didn't just walk into fights. I started a few. Looking back, I don't think it was to prove I could win—just to prove I was worth betting on.

And that instinct—to push, to test, to prove—became the foundation for everything.

I've always had a deep belief that I'm here to help people, especially the ones no one else bets on. That's probably what pushed me, at 29, to foster a 14-year-old boy who, on paper, had one of the toughest stories I'd ever seen. It wasn't the obvious move. But I've never been wired for obvious. I'm drawn to complexity. And I've learned to tell the difference between messy and hopeless. There's a big one.

It's why the word *no* barely registers. If someone tells me something can't be done, I hear an invitation to explore. That mindset helped me flip the security industry on its head and navigate high-stakes bodyguard work for A-list names like Ringo Starr, Nicole Kidman, and Donald Trump.

I launched Source Security with a hustler's mindset and a simple but powerful vision: to deliver better, more personalized security services. But it didn't take me long to realize what was really holding the industry back: midlevel management and a lack of culture. It slowed everything down. It disconnected decision-makers from the front lines. And worst of all, it stripped people of any real sense of purpose.

Security was an old-school industry, weighed down by bureaucracy and stuck in outdated ways. Innovation was actively ignored.

So I flipped the model and the org chart on their heads.

I put power in the hands of the guards. I gave them ownership, autonomy, and the ability to make real decisions. It wasn't some grand master plan. I just saw an opening to challenge the status quo.

And just like that, everything changed. People stepped up. They took pride in their work. They set a new standard and delivered in a way the industry had never seen.

What started as a business experiment grew to a staff of 3,500 across Canada and turned into a proven system built on trust, empowerment, and accountability. We weren't just cutting costs or increasing efficiency; we were creating a culture that actually worked.

Source Security exited with a 24x multiple to the largest company in the US (and now the largest globally), Allied Universal. That success pushed me to write two books, *Outrageous Empowerment* and *Scaling Culture*, and launch a master class and a podcast, and it introduced me to an incredible network of thinkers, builders, and disruptors. But I wasn't done.

I was looking for my next mountain to climb. And affordable housing was staring me in the face. I didn't need to be a real estate expert to see what was missing. What I needed was what I had always relied on: a deep understanding of people, a hunger to challenge the status quo, and a willingness to fight for change.

And this was personal.

I knew what it was like to struggle with housing. I knew the feeling of having bad credit, of being turned away, of knowing the system was stacked against you. And when I took a closer look at the affordable housing industry, I saw what I had seen in security years before: a system built on outdated thinking, riddled with inefficiencies, and completely disconnected from the people it was supposed to serve.

Case in point: landlords love the word *tenant*. It's distant and impersonal, a label that makes it easier to ignore the fact that the person renting from you is a *customer*—someone paying you for a service.

Real estate might be the only industry where the people you serve aren't called customers. In retail, hospitality, tech, you name it, they're customers. Imagine going to a restaurant and being called a "plate user." You'd laugh—or leave. But in housing, that kind of distance has somehow been accepted as the standard.

We don't use the word *tenant*. We say *customer* because that's what they are. When you start seeing people as customers, the whole industry shifts. You stop thinking, *How do I keep them from bothering me?* and start asking, *What else can I do to serve them?*

That's the foundation of VIDA.

We do more than buy buildings to protect affordable housing for Canadians. We create communities. Opportunities. Our model is about investing in people. We invest in our customers, help them build skills, give them a reason to take pride in where they live, and treat them with dignity and respect.

And when that happens, they don't just show up—*they step into their gifts* and lead in ways we're proud to make possible.

And it works.

That same question—*What else can we do for our customers?*—became our compass. It's what's kept customers at the centre and pushed us to evolve the model from the inside out.

And the answer? It wasn't some energy efficiency upgrade. Not an AI tool or the latest proptech app.

It was people—hiding in plain sight, right behind the doors of our buildings. That insight led to two of our biggest breakthroughs: the Building Ambassador model and the Community Contractor program.

Today, Building Ambassadors are the glue of VIDA communities. They welcome new customers, keep operations running smoothly, and flag issues before those problems spiral. They show units, handle light repairs, and help protect affordability by educating customers on things like waste sorting and smart utility use. More than anything, they build connection by hosting events, sharing updates, and making sure people feel seen, heard, and part of something bigger.

We took the same approach with repairs and maintenance, which plague the industry. We built scalable programs that gave everyday people—our own customers—the tools to lead, to earn, and to build real skills like painting, installing drywall, and caulking right in their own communities. Through the Community Contractor program, customers roll up their sleeves and get to work, tackling unit turns, common areas, and any non-warranty repairs. This led to lower operating costs and prouder communities.

You'll see how both programs evolved over time, but they started with one simple belief: the best people to lead a community are already living in it.

So we doubled down, investing in the people inside our buildings. Today, most of our key roles operate from within the communities themselves.

Because if we were going to reinvent this thing, what better place to start than right inside the buildings? We're creating safe, clean, proud communities from the ground up.

The way I see it, you can either complain about the system or you can change it. We chose the latter. And we're only just getting started.

It began in 2018 with one run-down 12-unit building. Today, VIDA has over 2,800 units and is transforming mismanaged buildings into thriving communities across Canada. We've redefined what it means to be a landlord. We've empowered residents in ways no one else has (and we're not stopping). Our goal is 10,000 units by 2027. And beyond that, we want to take this model global because every city, every country, has people who deserve better.

Freezing our first building and exterminating the cockroaches was a declaration. A line in the sand. If we were going to reinvent workforce housing, we had to be willing to do things differently, to take risks, to challenge everything that had been accepted as the status quo of affordable housing. VIDA wasn't just an idea. It was a necessity.

And look, I'm Canadian. We've got a rap for being humble and polite, sometimes to a fault. But fixing a crisis like affordable housing demands boldness. Urgency. We need to act like the problem is ours to solve because it is.

The gloves are off.

And I'm all in.

VIDA's model proves you can still generate profit while driving purpose and social impact. What follows is the real story—no filters, no fluff. You'll see how we discovered our business. Where we stumbled. Where we adapted. How we turned run-down buildings into thriving, innovative, resident-led communities. How we fought skepticism, setbacks, and systems designed to keep people stuck.

And how each challenge helped us sharpen our focus, not just on what worked but on what could truly scale.

Most importantly, you'll see the people—the customers, Community Contractors, Building Ambassadors, and Team Captains, along with those in Building Services and the Support Centre, and countless other partners who made VIDA what it is today.

Because this is bigger than a story about affordable housing and real estate. It's about reinvention. And it started on the inside, right where this industry never thought to look.

And if you think freezing a building was bold, just wait until you see what came next.

CHAPTER 2

Cracks in the Foundation

REINVENTING ANYTHING STARTS WITH ASKING THE BIG questions. For me, it took hitting rock bottom in the security industry to finally ask them. The good news is that the formula is simple. Ask bold questions. Work relentlessly. Build a world-class culture. And execute.

My first venture into real estate began when I was 21. I bought my first apartment building along with some commercial properties, small single-family homes, and duplexes. But the real entrance to multifamily housing happened in early 2018, right after I sold my security company. I bought a 12-unit building in Halifax with my good friend, Canadian actor and comedian Shaun Majumder. He was looking for investment opportunities, and when I pitched the idea to him, he believed in me.

The building wasn't in great shape. It was 50% vacant, and the mix of tenants was, well, less than 50% ideal. Still, I figured with my background in security, I could handle it. So I tapped into my old roots like I was about to run crowd control at a sold-out Rolling Stones concert—80,000 people, chaos in the air, and me at the centre. I was fired up and ready for action.

What I didn't expect was how much it would test me and how clearly it would show the path forward.

The building was completely neglected. Eggs smeared across the hallways, diapers thrown from windows, spray-painted walls, gaping holes in the drywall, and front doors torn off. Literally zero security to speak of.

That was when it hit me (thankfully not a diaper or an egg): there was an opportunity here, and it involved more than fixing buildings. It was about rethinking the whole damn system.

To truly change things, we had to look deeper. It wasn't enough to simply fix what was broken physically; we had to address the invisible cracks that ran through the entire system.

The affordable housing industry was outdated and broken. The landlord-tenant relationship was purely transactional. Landlords fixed the bare minimum (some didn't even do that), collected rent, and evicted tenants who fell behind. That was the entire relationship. No trust, no engagement, no community. Just friction.

My initial focus was on the physical repairs: fixing walls, patching roofs, and replacing broken appliances. Yet it didn't take long for me to realize something far more critical: the spaces we were repairing weren't just walls and floors; they were homes, places where people lived, worked, and raised families. I started by breaking it down: what were the key pain points, from the customer's perspective? What was stopping this from being a safe, livable home?

First: security. In affordable housing, landlords rarely invest in added security. They don't change locks when tenants move out. It's too costly. That leaves ex-tenants and whoever they gave keys to with access. It's a major risk. And when people don't feel safe, their pride disappears. Survival kicks in. The goal becomes simple: get in, and get out.

Second: cleanliness. When pride is gone, so is care. People stop cleaning up after themselves, stop reporting issues, stop caring. Neglected hallways and common areas and overflowing garbage bins send a clear message: no one gives a damn. And when that's the signal, everyone follows suit.

Third: amenities. Newer buildings boast high-end gyms, pools, and entertainment spaces. In contrast, older affordable housing properties often offer little to nothing in terms of amenities.

Fourth (and the most unorthodox): opportunity. Traditional affordable housing and real estate models often place little emphasis on upward mobility. The focus is on providing housing but not necessarily creating opportunities for personal growth or contribution. As a result, many residents find themselves in a cycle of renting and surviving rather than thriving.

That last one struck a chord. I had seen the power of giving people ownership and purpose back in my security business. We had eliminated middle management and empowered frontline staff to take on leadership roles. It changed everything. Why couldn't that work here too? But this time, the frontliners weren't employees. They were tenants. The customers.

In the security business we had a process called insourcing. We had access to so many full- and part-time employees who, although they had signed up to be security guards, no doubt had other untapped passions and skills. With the turnaround strategy of decentralizing and removing midlevel management, we needed to tap into our people to take the model to the next level. Insourcing was key to making that happen.

We needed our books reconciled, and this happened to be our next insourcing project. During a conversation with one of our security guards out in Burnaby, British Columbia, who had more accounting accolades than most of our accounting department combined, I had a realization. He had been a CFO in India but couldn't put it to work here in Canada. That struck me. Here was a guy with a ton of potential but no opportunity to use it.

That was when it clicked: why not give people like him the chance to contribute and build the business? It worked. Previously, bank reconciliation was typically four to five months behind, but we now had it completed every week for a much lower cost. More importantly, this gave our team members an increased sense of ownership, value, and purpose.

I realized that in affordable housing, each unit holds untapped potential. Who knows the skills, talents, and experiences of the customers behind those doors? What I did know for sure was that no one was knocking to find out.

My ADHD brain was now in full overdrive, like 1,000 popcorn kernels popping at once with this one question: *What if you had to restart the affordable housing industry from scratch?*

Instead of just fixing buildings, we'd transform them from the inside out.

The top priority was security, and I was in my element. We went all out, installing fob access and high-end security cameras—things you'd expect in luxury apartments but that were unheard of in affordable housing. When people feel safe, they feel more confident in their surroundings. And let's be clear: this wasn't only about keeping people safe; it was about setting the tone that this place and its people were worth investing in.

Then came cleanliness. I hired a single mom—one of the tenants—who had been throwing used diapers out her windows. In exchange for a small rent credit, I asked her if she would be interested in keeping the place clean. She went above and beyond, and the transformation was incredible. She quickly went from a "problem tenant" to a problem-solver and key contributor. Suddenly, the building looked better than anything else on the block.

With the basics in place, next came amenities. The basement was a junk-filled mouse den. I cleared it out and repurposed the space, cobbling together a small gym with secondhand equipment. I added a book exchange and built a community garden. Slowly but surely, the energy started shifting and people started taking pride in where they lived.

Then came the game changer: opportunity.

This was about helping people step into their gifts, and it started the way most good ideas do: with listening. As I had for our insourcing process at my previous company, Source Security, I started asking residents, "Can you paint? Fix things? Help with maintenance?" The response was overwhelming. They were eager to contribute. So we gave them a shot. Painting hallways. Fixing doors. Cleaning common areas. We offered rent credits or extra income. I saw more than just contractors. I saw potential. If we could unlock the talent already living in our buildings, we could build stronger communities from the inside out.

And just like that, the Community Contractor program started taking shape—people helping build something bigger than themselves. A thriving, clean, safe, and proud community.

Some people wanted to help but didn't yet have the skills. So we ran DIY workshops on weekends and in the evenings. We'd gather in a unit that needed turning. One corner became a painting zone, another for drywall, another for caulking. And when someone crossed the finish line and could work solo, we'd celebrate them. Tell their story. Recognize them publicly.

Eventually, we built an internal search app so other buildings could find and hire local Community Contractors. It worked beautifully in Halifax. But like anything, the model had to evolve as we scaled. What worked in one city didn't always translate. Its true potential—and some challenges—still lay ahead.

* * *

We were just starting to scratch the surface of creating a new model built on four pillars: security, cleanliness, community, and opportunity. The focus was no longer on making the buildings work and keeping them running; it was on reimagining everything about them.

With a foundation starting to take shape, I was ready to take it to the next level when an even bigger challenge emerged: a 100-unit portfolio in Halifax. The price? Almost identical to what I had sold my security company for. That was both daunting and exhilarating.

The buildings were some of the worst in Halifax: four buildings, three condemned and one still occupied but riddled with crime. One was the most dangerous building in Canada in 2015, logging over 215 police calls in a single year (let's call it 215 Police Call Drive). Officers wouldn't even send regular patrol units. It was considered too high risk.

The financials were just as bad. The properties carried massive debt, and the bank had no idea how bad things were. They had been sold based on false appraisals, inflated rent rolls, and fictitious valuations. While most real estate investors saw a disaster, I saw potential.

I approached the sellers and the bank with a bold offer: "I'll take the debt. No premium. Just give me the properties, and I'll fix them." At the same time, I pitched Nova Scotia

Housing on a plan to bring the units back to market. I met some resistance, as government programs typically fund new builds, not renovations. But I argued that these buildings had been vacant for so long that restoring them was as valuable as adding new supply.

People like Barbara Kjarbo made all the difference. She was instrumental in helping secure long-term affordability agreements in exchange for funding. Without her, the deal might never have happened. She took time to understand the vision, tour the buildings, and meet with customers.

Her hands-on approach and expertise helped us navigate the complex regulatory landscape and build a partnership that was critical to our success. She was very interested in our proof of concept: a model where the private sector and government could collaborate to create real solutions for working-class Canadians living in affordable housing.

One of the biggest hurdles in affordable housing isn't building more; it's keeping what already exists. Many government programs in Canada are designed to create new stock for private, nonprofit, or community developers. But there's nothing to preserve the 800,000-plus deeply affordable units already in place. When these buildings are sold to "renovictors," value-adders and other investors who typically hike rents, those units are lost forever.

We needed millions in capital to repair the buildings. They were beyond run-down: frozen pipes, collapsed ceilings, mould, rats, cockroaches, bedbugs, you name it.

But I was all in. I invested my own money, and Nova Scotia Housing provided $50,000 per unit in exchange for keeping rents affordable for 15 years. It was a win-win. This was how we could scale while keeping rents low and improving the living conditions for tenants.

As a lifelong leaner, I was enrolled in the Entrepreneurial Masters Program (EMP) at MIT. That was where I learned about the power of focus.

Now, for someone with ADHD, focus is a bit like a mythical creature: always just a bit elusive and out of reach. I'm more used to my brain hopping from one idea to another at lightning speed, like a squirrel on an espresso binge. And don't get me started on my dyslexia. Reading through complicated business theories is like decoding an ancient language.

I was sitting at the EMP when Verne Harnish, my friend and mentor, and now an advisor to VIDA, offered some game-changing advice: "If you want to build a unicorn like Airbnb or Uber, find 10% of an industry where you know you can dominate. Then focus on 70% of that slice."

For me, that clicked. You don't take down an entire industry by swinging wild. I didn't need to wrangle my chaotic brain into submission; I just had to give it a single lane to run in. So I channelled my energy and creativity into one thing: taking over that slice of the market and owning it. You find the weak spot, the slice no one else is owning, and you focus like hell.

For me, that lane was affordable housing—wide open, overlooked, and ready to be reimagined. I wanted to go deeper and deliver better than anyone else. That's where the transformation starts.

Why does it work? Because focus wins. When you go narrow and deep, you get closer to the customer. You understand their pain. You speak their language. You solve problems others don't even see. Suddenly, you're not just in the game; you *are* the game.

That's how you scale strategically. You dominate one slice, build systems, and earn trust—and then expand.

This new perspective helped me refine my approach. I realized that by narrowing our focus and dominating one slice of the market, we could build something truly special. No longer would I be the chief distraction officer, chasing every opportunity. It was time to become the chief focus officer. I could go deeper and focus on what mattered most: providing affordable, quality housing for working-class Canadians.

The focus: workforce housing.

As I delved into the industry, I saw a clear gap: naturally occurring affordable housing, or what the US calls "workforce housing."

In 2018, "affordable housing" had a stigma. It was associated with neglect and had a rap of being charity-driven. But in the US, workforce housing described homes for everyday working-class people—nurses, grocery clerks, single parents. That resonated with me.

Our tenants weren't helpless. They weren't looking for handouts. They were working-class Canadians, and they deserved respect. So we adopted the term *workforce housing*, and we've used it ever since.

These were older buildings, mostly from the 1970s, '80s, and '90s, and were home to people like frontline workers, who were the backbone of every community. But the landlord-tenant relationship was broken—cold and transactional, without trust. I knew this had to change.

I imagined a new dynamic where tenants and landlords were co-stakeholders in the community. It was a radical idea, but I believed it could work. But where did I start? You can't just expect someone to care like a partner given the history and tension in landlord-tenant relationships. Trust had to be built from the ground up.

As I studied the industry, I noticed a pattern. Nonprofits were doing good work but struggling to scale. Slumlords didn't care. Institutional players—REITs, pension funds, value-adders—owned everything from trailer parks to luxury condos but often managed them through third parties with no real connection to the tenants.

There was no alignment. It was stale, male-dominated, and soulless. It needed a new voice. A new brand. Something human. Something warm. Something that said, "You belong here."

I thought back to my travels. Fifty-six countries, and the ones that stayed with me were the places that made me feel alive and at home, like I had been there before in another life. Latin cultures especially exuded warmth, kindness, a sense of life.

That was when it clicked. One word: VIDA. Spanish for "life."

It felt right. And just like that, VIDA Living was born.

* * *

Great at Work by Morten Hansen describes the concept of P-squared, or purpose and passion. When you combine what you love with your reason for being, you become unstoppable. That hit home.

By 37, I knew my purpose. I'd always loved helping people. That was the through line. I have no qualms about jumping on a call if a high school kid from South Africa has a follow-up question after listening to my *Scaling Culture* podcast.

And my passion was turning stale, broken industries upside down. That was what lit me up in the security business. That was what I wanted again.

But this time I wanted to build something that made a real impact. Something that gave people a shot. I'd seen how real estate treated people like transactions. Commodities. I hated that.

If I was going to do this, it had to be purpose-driven. That purpose would carry me through the grind—the long nights, the mental toll, the risks. And believe me, it gets hard. Starting something new always does. Your mental health takes a toll. Your time disappears. You question everything. But when you know you're building something that matters, you find another gear.

For me, this was it.

I'd found the intersection of purpose, passion, and real-world impact. I had the vision. The name. The model. The fire. But to really scale VIDA, we had to make one more thing work: profit. We had to prove that this wasn't charity. It was smart business. We had to make the math work, at scale, over time.

That was when the doubters started to show up.

He doesn't know what he's doing. He's in over his head. This is a terrible idea.

And to be fair, they weren't entirely wrong. Looking back, the buildings were in rough shape. The tenants had their challenges. The financials were messy. But I knew that if we could make it work there, it could work anywhere.

And it did. Through relentless focus, a foundation of core pillars, a strong team, and a clear vision, we took the infamous 215 Police Call Drive from being one of the most dangerous buildings in the country to being a functioning, thriving community.

That was when I knew this wasn't about one building or one city. The same questions that led me to push the boundaries in the security space had the potential to reshape an entire industry.

Ask bold questions. Work relentlessly. Build a world-class culture. And execute.

What if we stopped treating housing as a transaction and started treating it as a foundation for opportunity? What if we built communities instead of just buildings?

What if reinvention wasn't the exception but the expectation?

I knew I was onto something. Now it was time to test the model on the building next door.

Would the model hold up? There was only one way to find out.

CHAPTER 3

Pressure, Patience, and a Little Ketchup

IF YOU THOUGHT 215 POLICE CALL DRIVE WAS BAD, THE neighbouring building we acquired was a full-on war zone. This was just one building in a tangled, messy portfolio of about 100 units. Most of it was unlivable, broken, or outright condemned. But I saw what others missed: potential.

Complex? Absolutely. But complex doesn't scare me. It excites me.

When things get messy, most people walk away. I lean in.

One day, I was standing outside the building with the police, getting ready for a walk-through. The previous owner had told me there was still a superintendent on-site. Sure enough, a guy walked up, oozing confidence. "The building's great," he said. "The tenants? Wonderful."

And then we heard it. "Low battery. Low battery." The guy pulled up his pant leg to reveal an ankle monitor. The cops looked at me. "That's your super?"

"Nope," I said. "Not anymore."

Back when I was still considering the deal, I called John Risley, a legendary Halifax entrepreneur and multibillion-dollar builder. I told him what I was looking at. I also told him what everyone else had been telling me since I sold my company: "Don't do anything for two years."

John didn't buy that advice. He said, "The best time to do a deal is when you don't need to do a deal."

And he was right.

When you're not desperate, you have leverage. You can negotiate anything. You don't chase. You choose. That mindset gave me the confidence to move forward.

The buildings were still a disaster, but I was all in.

* * *

Just like next door, regular police wouldn't even enter the building. If they did, they went undercover. That was how bad it was.

The building still had people living in it—about 30% of the units were occupied—but it would be a stretch to call it "livable." The real challenge wasn't even just the building; it was the human element. Drug dealers moved in and out like it was their office, and prostitution was out in the open. The place was dangerous.

So how could we bring in our pillars—security, cleanliness, community, opportunity—without making this place feel like a prison?

At first, I thought a police satellite office might help. In some rough neighbourhoods, even a small visible presence can make a big difference. So I called up the local police.

Their response? Highly unlikely.

I couldn't believe it. I was offering them a free space, a

coffee machine, and an opportunity to support the community. All I was asking for was a uniform in the hallway once in a while.

Despite their reluctance, I sat down with the watch commander, and something started to feel off. That's when I knew: this wasn't the right move. A police office inside the building would send the wrong message to future customers. It would do the exact opposite of what we were trying to achieve with our security pillar. It would scream, "This place is dangerous. Don't come here unless you must." After all, when you're always surrounded by law enforcement, you start to feel like you're the problem, even when you're not.

I flashed back to a trip I'd taken with the Young Presidents' Organization (YPO) to Moscow. I walked into a shopping mall that had metal detectors, security checks, and pat-downs. As a customer just trying to shop, my instinct was to turn around and leave. I had that same gut reaction now: this wasn't the kind of welcome we wanted to create.

So I scrapped the police office idea. It was the right call. Instead, I had to manage the building as it was—drug dens, roaches, and all.

I began knocking on doors. My approach was to get to know them, find out if they respected the property, if they were a danger to the community. One unit I'll never forget. I opened the door, and cockroaches rained from the ceiling. Hundreds of them crawled everywhere.

I knew some tenants couldn't stay, but it wasn't about moving them out; it was about moving them forward. The building wasn't a place anyone could truly call home in its current state, and what they really needed was a fresh start. It felt like running a matchmaking service for people in crisis. I'd meet with them, learn what they needed, and set up appointments with shelters and landlords. It wasn't fast, and it wasn't easy. But it mattered.

One tenant was a known drug dealer, confirmed by both the police and the activity at the building. We knew this person wasn't a good fit for the community we were trying to build, and it became critical to figure out how to get them to leave.

We tried the straightforward approach: asking the tenant to leave. We explained that we didn't think they were a good fit for the building and offered to let them break their lease without any penalties. The tenant agreed, saying they'd be out by the first of the month. But sure enough, the next month came, and no movement. No sign of leaving.

Later, I got a call from our construction manager, who confirmed that the tenant still hadn't left. This went on for months. We were getting paid, but we were certainly getting played.

I knew it was time to get creative.

Dealing with a tenant who knew the system better than we did was like playing a rigged game. They understood every loophole, every technicality, and they used it all to their advantage. We brought in the rental board. Nothing. We tried the police. No luck. Every time we thought we were making progress, they were already one step ahead. They had played this game at least 70 times before. This wasn't their first rodeo; they were a pro at squatting and manipulating the system.

We threw everything at the problem. We offered money. We made arrangements. We tried to negotiate a peaceful exit that worked for everyone. And every single time, they broke their word. It was exhausting. The pressure was building, and we knew this was about the bigger picture. If we couldn't hold the line here, it would undermine everything we were working so hard to build with the rest of the community.

Here was where my street smarts and creativity really kicked in. The tenant had a known fear of pests. Anytime they thought there was a pest issue, they panicked and demanded immediate action. So I came up with a plan. I sent them a text, pretending to send a message to our pest control contact instead.

Hi, Johnny. We've got a major problem here with rats. A rat bit one of our plumbers, and he had to go to the hospital. It's a serious issue. We need all the support we can get to fix the problem.

I quickly followed up with:

Oops, sorry, wrong person. Please ignore.

The reaction was immediate. The tenant panicked and called, demanding that we take care of the rat issue. We leaned in to the strategy, posting signs around the building stating that a plumber and four workers had been bitten by rats and warning everyone to stay in well-lit areas. Then came the kicker: a sign by the front door that read, *Missing: Mitzi the cat. Last seen near the laundry room.* No one said she was dead, but everyone assumed she was. Mitzi became a legend overnight.

The tenant was clearly rattled, but we knew we needed one final push.

This was street smarts versus street smarts. And they'd been playing this game a lot longer than I had. But I don't back down from a challenge. We weren't going to lose. We just had to think differently, roll up our sleeves, and outmanoeuvre. And that was exactly what we did. Luckily for me, I get extremely excited trying to solve these complex situations. This is where my neurodivergent superpowers kick in!

I told the construction manager to go out and buy a small, grey stuffed animal. Then I asked him to cut off one of its legs, place it in a rat trap, and smear ketchup around it to look like an injury. He looked at me like I was crazy, but he followed through and set it right outside the tenant's apartment door.

Sure enough, within 24 hours, the tenant was gone. Moved out without a word. No notice. No noise. Just gone.

That whole situation taught us an important lesson: sometimes the traditional approach doesn't work. But if you understand what matters to someone—what they fear, what motivates them—you can guide the outcome without force.

We stayed stubborn on vision—protecting the community—but flexible on execution. It was about doing what worked. We got the outcome we needed and kept the community safe, all through a creative solution to a tough problem.

And then I started hearing whispers about bedbugs in another building within the portfolio. Was this payback for the false alarm we'd triggered? Had the real pest problem been lurking behind the walls all along? I couldn't shake the feeling that something more serious was waiting for us.

* * *

Real estate is full of surprises. You never think your next big hire will be a guy with dogs who sniff out bedbugs. But that's exactly how I met Brian, the Bedbug Detective.

The whispers quickly became a gut feeling I couldn't shake. Pest control told me I was paranoid. After all, the building was empty. "No people, no food, no bedbugs," they said. I told them I'd found a guy with dogs trained to sniff out bedbug infestations for $300 a pop. They laughed like I'd gone off the deep end.

"You mean a pet detective who's also a pest detective?"

We booked him.

The first dog stepped into the building and sat—15 times. Each sit marked a different spot. Each spot, a signal: bedbugs alive and well, living in the walls. I marked them all with tape, starting to feel like a lunatic.

I told the handler I wasn't buying it. So in came the second dog. This one scratched every single area where the first dog had sat. Every spot.

Still skeptical, I asked for one more test. The handler handed me a bedbug in a spice jar. "Hide it anywhere," he said. I walked up to the third floor, kicked a hole in the wall, stashed the bug, and then kicked more holes just to throw them off. The dog came in, sniffed around, and walked straight to the wall I'd hidden the bug behind. Scratched like crazy.

Game over. I was sold. From that day on, Brian and his dogs became part of the VIDA team.

Renovations at the building were brutal. It was a shell, condemned by the police for over a year. No one would give fixed quotes. Everything was time and materials. Every wall we opened revealed another nightmare: mould, asbestos, ancient plumbing disasters, you name it.

Nova Scotia Housing had kicked in some money, and I had set aside personal funds to get going. But we blew through all of it. Fast. I had buildings full of cockroaches and bedbugs, zero rental income, and over $5 million in debt with the Bank of Montreal.

To make things even more interesting, I had a one-year-old at home. Georgia.

I was almost completely out of money. And I was terrified. This was the nightmare: the entrepreneur who exits, only to crash and burn a few years later. I felt it. I was living it.

Desperate, I went back to the bank, specifically to Justin Scully. Justin had been a bartender at Oasis nightclub in Halifax, where Source Security had the contract for the door. Years later, he landed at BMO and helped me secure my first $1,000 loan.

Now I needed half a million. I sat across from him and said, "Justin, I took on this debt to bail you guys out. Now I need you to bail me out."

He made it happen. That $500,000 loan was more than just survival. It was ignition. It kept VIDA alive. It gave us just enough fuel to push through the rubble and build something real. Something that mattered.

After the renovations were finally complete and there wasn't a cockroach or bedbug in sight, we decided to mark the milestone with our first open house. It was time to invite the public in.

Just a few years earlier, no one in their right mind would have walked through those doors. Now we were opening them wide. It felt like a big moment. The work had been relentless, the pressure heavy. But we made it.

The morning of the open house, I walked into the show unit to take one last look. I stepped onto the hardwood floor, and my heart sank.

Scratches everywhere.

We only did a light sand and a fresh coat of varnish, but the marks and dings were still visible. I looked closer. The baseboards weren't even. There were tiny blemishes on the walls. Panic kicked in. We were asking $850 a month for a two-bedroom, heat and hot water included. But how could I ask anyone to live here, knowing what this place used to be and now seeing these imperfections?

The address still carried a heavy reputation. At one point, I even considered applying to change the name of the street just to give it a fresh start. As people started arriving, I stood in the unit, heart racing. It was a Saturday afternoon. The sun was out. I was anxious. Embarrassed. Then the first tenant walked in.

He looked around, took a deep breath, and said, "Oh my god." I braced myself. My stomach dropped. This was it. It was over just as fast as it started.

Then he smiled. "I love it. *I love it.*"

I couldn't believe what I was hearing. *He loved it.*

That moment shifted everything. I'd been looking at the unit through my own lens, seeing every scratch, every imperfection. But the tenant saw something completely different: a fresh start. Stability. Affordability. *Possibility.*

That was when it clicked: *I am not the customer.*

From that day on, we stopped using the word *tenants.* We use *customers.* Because that's what they are. Not obligations. Not numbers. Customers—with choice, with value, with potential gifts to step into.

We also scrapped the word *unit.* This was more than another rental. This was someone's home. It wasn't just a word swap; it was a statement. A mindset.

We were no longer showing units for tenants. We were showing homes for customers. We weren't just fixing buildings. We were fixing the relationship between landlords and the people they serve. We were rebuilding trust. And with that, everything counts, even language.

That open house wasn't the end of a renovation. It marked the start of something far bigger than I could have imagined.

PART 2

The Climb Begins

CHAPTER 4

Stubborn on Vision

GROWTH OFTEN REVEALS YOUR LIMITS—NOT JUST IN money or time but in resilience. By the time we had just over 100 units, VIDA was no longer just a startup story. It was a test of what we stood for. Part 2 of VIDA's journey was about resilience and learning how to stand in the middle of a mess and figure out how to clean it up when everyone else had walked away. We had to be stubborn on vision and flexible on execution.

We weren't a big player...yet. But we were in deep. And it was time to see how much risk, how much mess, and how much uncertainty we could stomach. Turns out that it was a lot.

In early 2019, with that portfolio under our belt, it was time for another acquisition. One day, a customer mentioned an older gentleman named Mr. Hope who owned several buildings in the neighbourhood. He was in his mid- to late 80s. I heard he could still be seen out there salting his own driveway. "You should talk to him," the customer said. "He might be ready to sell."

Sure enough, a few days later while I was at the property, I spotted Mr. Hope outside, right where I was told I'd find him: spreading salt across his driveway. I walked up and introduced myself, explaining that I had bought the building next door.

Mr. Hope was very kind, and we struck up a conversation. I asked about his plans for the buildings, whether he intended to keep them or pass them on to his kids. He admitted that his kids weren't interested in the properties and that he might be open to selling, though he enjoyed keeping busy by tending to them. Admiring his dedication, I thought, *Here's a man in his late 80s, out here salting his driveway on blocks of ice.* It reminded me of what longevity in the industry could look like.

I told Mr. Hope I was interested in buying his buildings. He had three buildings: two 12-unit walk-ups and another a block over. I made an offer: $1.7 million for the properties. Then I asked if we had a deal. He laughed and told me, "You move way too fast for my liking. I'll need to talk to my wife first." When I asked if I could check back in three days, he replied, "If you wait three days, I won't even remember we met." We both had a good laugh.

Eventually, I purchased the buildings. While Mr. Hope was a great guy, he was struggling to operate his properties. Some customers were taking advantage of him, and the buildings had fallen into disrepair. When I did a walk-through before buying, I found a bird's nest in one of the kitchen cupboards. Birds had come in through the ventilation system and nested there.

There was also significant water damage. The roof was so bad that in some places, you could see the sky through the cracks. This was an "amenity upgrade" we hadn't planned for. But we jumped in, did the work, and brought it back to life.

The key to that deal wasn't money; it was trust. I didn't treat it like a transaction. I built a relationship. Everyone else had been knocking on his door for years, trying to buy his buildings. No one got through until we did. I brought him a turkey dinner. I showed up. I listened.

That connection unlocked the next phase for VIDA. That deal could've been the headline for this chapter.

Until one day Mr. Hope leaned in and said, "There's one more place I didn't mention."

It was a 20-unit side-by-side tucked away on a quiet street. A hidden gem not on the market and not in great shape. For a time, we dubbed it "Hopeful Lane," a nod to both the owner and the condition of the place.

Hopeful Lane had been overlooked for years—and for good reason. The ceiling was caving in. Water damage everywhere. But the real problem wasn't what we could see. It was what was buried underneath. Years earlier, a major oil spill had occurred on-site and had never been cleaned up. The kind of issue that scares lenders and buyers away. In our world, no environmental clearance means no financing. Full stop.

Could VIDA fix what everyone else had buried, both literally and figuratively?

* * *

This wasn't the kind of problem you outbid. It was one you had to outthink.

I offered to buy the property for $800,000, but with a twist. Mr. Hope owned it outright, so I proposed a vendor take-back mortgage for the full amount. The structure was simple: for every dollar I spent on environmental cleanup, I'd owe $1 less. If I spent $200,000, I'd owe $600,000. If I spent more than $800,000, I'd owe nothing but would be responsible for any additional costs myself. Risky, but clean.

Then we opened Pandora's box. The environmental firm told us the oil had seeped underground and down the street. It hadn't reached the water system, but it was close. The estimate to fix it was $1.5 million.

I panicked. I called the local water company and laid it out bluntly. "If you expect me to pay $1.5 million, I'll drop you off the keys, and you'll own this building." They knew the area. They certainly didn't want to own a property like this, and I made it clear: this was a zero-sum game unless we found common ground.

I offered them $10,000 to sign off on the issue. It wasn't even close to what they wanted, but it was all I could afford. And I told them our bigger vision. We were trying to preserve affordable housing in a community that hadn't seen real investment in decades. To my relief, they agreed.

But we weren't done yet. A neighbouring property had also been affected by the spill. Fixing that would have cost us hundreds of thousands more. We were already $600,000 deep on cleaning up Hopeless Lane and had no capacity for another half-million-dollar fix. I knew the owner was a long-term holder who planned to redevelop eventually. I made him a deal: I offered him $200,000 if he'd assume responsibility for his site. He said yes.

That was it. We had buy-in from the key stakeholders and clearance on the environmental side, and we were finally in the clear. In the end, we finished the entire cleanup with $17,000 to spare. Just enough to breathe. Barely. Still, we made it. And Hopeful Lane got a second chance.

Our lawyer managing the negotiations admitted we were way outside the typical playbook. "This isn't normal. I've never seen a deal structured like this."

Stubborn on vision. Flexible on execution.

To be honest, I was anxious the entire way through. There was always the chance we'd blow past the $800,000 cap, and I knew I couldn't take another hit like that. The whole experience made one thing painfully clear: I couldn't keep doing deals like this without stronger advisors—people who'd challenge me, push back, and help me make better decisions.

The big lesson? When the operational risks are high and the consequences irreversible, you have to slow down. Jeff Bezos calls these "one-way door" decisions—the kind you can't undo. That was exactly what this was. You move fast when the stakes are low. But when there's no going back, you stop, think, and make damn sure you get it right.

This was also about relationship building. With Mr. Hope. With the neighbours. With the people already living there. You can't bulldoze your way into trust. You need to earn it every time.

When you take over a neglected property, the instinct is to go full throttle, to fix everything fast, to prove you're different. But that's when you miss the land mines. The better approach is to pause, listen, and surround yourself with the right people. You need legal, environmental, and inspection experts before the deal, not after.

As an entrepreneur, I often default to "we'll figure it out." That mindset has carried me a long way, but there's a point where it stops being brave and starts being reckless. This was that point.

We needed that wake-up call. But we also needed a reminder of what we were capable of. And it came not long after, when we expanded across the bridge to the city of Dartmouth, Nova Scotia.

* * *

As we continued to expand, we found ourselves looking at a new property in Dartmouth. Courtney Sherlock, my partner at the time and a powerhouse entrepreneur, had scaled her veterinary company like a pro, sold, and even launched the Halifax Tides, the first Canadian professional women's soccer team. So naturally, the two of us thought, *How hard could a tiny 12-unit apartment building be?*

We were buzzing with excitement when we showed up for the tour, but something felt off the second we stepped inside. "Courtney, is it me, or is this place too clean?" I muttered.

"Right?" she replied, eyeing a mop bucket that had been conveniently left in the middle of the hallway like it was part of the decor. "Who leaves cleaning supplies out like they're staging a photo shoot?"

The floors were so shiny I could practically see my future in them. Every unit we walked into was immaculate—floors freshly mopped, countertops sparkling like someone had just run through with a professional cleaning crew seconds before we arrived. It felt staged, but not in the professional realtor kind of way. More like, *Don't look behind the curtain.*

Then we opened the door to a unit jammed with boxes to the ceilings and mismatched furniture—so much stuff we could barely squeeze inside. It was like stepping into a warehouse of failed IKEA experiments. "Whoa, what's the deal here?" I asked, turning to a customer who was conveniently hovering nearby.

"Oh, we just moved in!" they chirped, way too casually. "That's why it's a bit of a mess."

I side-eyed Courtney. Her face said everything: *I'm not buying it either.*

But we figured, *Hey, what's the worst that could happen?*

So we shook hands, signed the papers, and bought the building.

A few weeks later, the truth came out. I called Courtney, full sarcasm in my voice. "Court, you're gonna love this."

"Oh no," she groaned. "What now?"

"Turns out our friendly seller paid the customers fifty bucks each to make the place sparkle for our tour."

She didn't miss a beat. "And that couple who 'just moved in'?"

"Long-term customers. Hoarders. And the unit's infested with pests. Surprise!"

We couldn't help but laugh.

"So we basically bought a 12-unit magic trick," she said.

"Yup. Lesson learned: never trust floors that clean themselves."

From then on, I swore we'd never be duped like that again. We got serious about customer-focused due diligence. It's about thinking beyond spreadsheets. If you don't open cupboards, check closets, and peek behind couches, you're asking for trouble. You have to be in the building—see it, smell it, feel it. When you nail due diligence, the rest takes care of itself.

So when another opportunity popped up in Dartmouth, this time a set of 32 townhouses, we were ready. This was a different kind of acquisition for us. These were family-style homes, more of a neighbourhood than a typical apartment complex.

The day after we closed, I got a call from the office. A police officer had shown up asking to speak with me. He was the community liaison at the time. He's retired now, but I'll never forget that first meeting.

When I arrived, he introduced himself and got straight to it. "I'm here to meet the guy who just bought this place."

His brow furrowed. The concern in his voice was obvious. "Do you understand what you've walked into? Who are you? What's your background? Do you know how dangerous it is here?"

I was stunned. I thought we were taking on a fairly standard property. Now I was being told even the police avoided it. But of course, the challenge excited me. We had something to prove, and I was determined to turn it around.

One of the biggest challenges was a customer running a major drug operation out of his unit. Cars lined the street outside his place, coming and going like clockwork. It looked like the line for a ride at Disney World. The police wouldn't intervene, so we had to figure it out ourselves. I figured we'd seen this before—the staged rat, Mitzi the cat. I knew this wasn't about confrontation. It was about motivation.

I paid the customer a visit, introduced myself, and asked if we could talk privately in the basement. Once we were seated, I told him something in the hope that it would rattle him enough to leave. "The police have approached me about renting the unit across the street. They've offered a lot of money, and from a business perspective, I can't say no."

And just like that I could see the wheels turning. I didn't accuse him of anything directly, but I made it clear: the police were planning to be nearby. I told him that if he chose to leave, I'd let the police know I had no idea where he went. He looked at me, nodded, and said, "I'll be out in seven days." And just like that, a week later, he was gone—and the steady stream of traffic disappeared with him.

That reinforced something important: solving tough problems wasn't about force; it was about understanding the people inside the buildings and getting creative. We figured out how to get the wrong people out without resorting to drawn-out legal battles, and in doing so, we saved time and money and started to rebuild something stronger.

It felt like a clean sting. No force. No fight. No need to rat him out.

Of course, for every step forward, there were two steps back.

Next up? The actual rats.

* * *

The rat problem at the 32-unit townhouses was like something out of a horror movie. They were everywhere. We caught dozens of them every day, but they just kept coming. They chewed through front doors and burrowed their way into people's homes.

One customer sent me a video I'll never forget: a rat, bold as hell, scaling her glass patio door in the middle of the day. Not scurrying, not hiding. Just clinging there, mid-climb, like it paid rent. On the other side of the glass, she stood frozen, terrified. I remember staring at the screen and thinking, *You can't make this stuff up!*

We went all in and worked closely with pest control to put together a full strategy. We attacked the problem from the outside in: setting perimeter traps, sealing every potential entry point, and going unit by unit to find and eliminate the ones already inside. We even offered to buy every customer a cat. It was an intense, monthslong battle.

Eventually, we won. But the fear of them coming back never fully disappears. The thing about pests is that they don't care about postal codes. High-end neighbourhood or run-down complex—it doesn't matter. They go where they're allowed. And that's everywhere. It's all about how you care for your home. If it's neglected, they'll take over.

That's when it clicked: we weren't just buying properties.

We were inheriting stories. Reputations. Neglect. Problems. The previous owners had left the property to deteriorate, and customers expected us to fix it—fast.

It brought me back to how we made the leap from tenant to customer, but how did we get to co-stakeholder? We knew it went back to the language we used and how we communicated. So we changed our tone and started being up-front with the customers: "Here's what we've found. We need your help. If there's something we don't know about, tell us. We will make a plan together."

That made a huge difference. It built trust. It made us partners, not landlords, and set the stage for a co-stakeholder relationship to flourish. And that was the key to everything that would come next—VIDA's platform expansion.

This chapter of VIDA's growth was a flicker of progress—what happens when sparks catch. We were transforming properties and building proof that affordable housing could work, even in the toughest places—and that if you get the model right, you don't have to fear the next mess. You just need to be ready for it.

There were moments I questioned everything: my decisions, my ability, even the vision itself. It felt like running uphill through mud, dragging years of neglect behind us. But then I'd see a customer step up, a building start to shift, a street begin to breathe again. It was slow. It was messy. But it was happening.

Those flickers of progress kept me going. They reminded me that this was bigger than real estate or turning a profit. This was changing lives, changing neighbourhoods and an industry. Anytime doubt crept in, I reminded myself, *Nothing worth building is easy. If it were, someone would've done it already.*

And we were learning about where our model could

thrive. Townhouses, for example, didn't fit. The individual-ized nature—separate lawns, scattered responsibilities—made it nearly impossible to uphold VIDA's cleanliness pillar. In the end, we chose to sell in the name of focus.

With every setback we not only survived; we got sharper. Every mess resulted in a new playbook. Each time we out-thought the problem instead of outspending it, we proved we had more tools in the toolbox than we realized. And each time we brought community members into the solution, the turnaround stuck.

And the next time someone told me "That place is too far gone," I smiled, rolled up my sleeves, and thought, *Perfect.*

CHAPTER 5

Opportunity Knocks

FROM THE OUTSIDE, IT LOOKED LIKE WE WERE STILL just acquiring buildings. But inside, something else was happening: the early architecture of a platform where the people inside the buildings weren't just tenants but future contributors and co-stakeholders. And Sandra became one of the clearest early signals of that shift.

When I got the notice that the building was being sold, my stomach dropped. I'd lived at 30 Spring Hill for over 15 years. For 10 of those, I was the superintendent. I knew every crack in the wall, every neighbour's name, and every leak that needed patching. But when buildings change hands, everything changes with them. I'd seen it before. Usually, it wasn't good.

I assumed the buyer would be a big corporate landlord—maybe a REIT, maybe someone from out of province. So I did what anyone would do: I googled who it might possibly be. That was when I came across a CBC article by Elizabeth Chiu about VIDA and their turnaround of some condemned buildings in Halifax,

Nova Scotia. It wasn't just about fixing things; it was about building something better. I thought, *This guy's cracked the code. This is what housing's been missing.* And for a second, I let myself hope, *What if VIDA bought this place?*

Then came the notice: a group was touring the building.

I braced myself. But when Ron walked in, I knew him immediately. Not from some past interaction but from the article. I smiled, maybe too big. He looked at me like he was trying to place me. But I already knew who he was. And for the first time in weeks, I felt a flicker of hope.

But hope wasn't the only thing I felt. I had questions. Would I still have a role? Would I be replaced? Would they fix the building or flip it? Could I keep doing this? And did they even want me to?

When Sandra smiled at me that day, I thought we'd met before. Turned out that she recognized me from the media coverage. That smile was a signal: she believed in what we were building. And before long, she became a key part of the team.

We kept her in the superintendent role, and she played a huge part in stabilizing the building during the transition. Over time, we got to know each other better, and it became clear she had even more to offer. Her years as a customer and superintendent gave her an incredible window into what it looks like when people can't—or won't—pay rent. She always kept meticulous notes and thorough documentation. She used to joke that she wanted to be a teacher and that she had a side hustle as a detective.

So when an opening came up on our finance admin team,

we didn't need to look far. The right person was already in front of us.

Sandra joined our finance admin group and started running accounts receivable across the country. Who better for the job than someone who'd lived the experience, someone with real empathy who understood the challenges customers face and the evidence needed to resolve them? Naturally, she helped us manage tenancy hearings and shape strategy.

A lot of companies keep an empty chair in the boardroom to represent the customer. Jeff Bezos famously did this at Amazon. At VIDA, we do it differently. We put customers in the chair. And not just in frontline roles. We hire customers from within for finance, admin, and operational roles too.

Stories like this are proof that the best way to serve our communities is to build them with the people who live in them. Sandra didn't just join the team. She helped evolve the company from the inside out.

Remember that dream she had about becoming a teacher? At one of our quarterly planning sessions, she pitched the idea of the VIDA Bursary Program. She knew firsthand how hard it can be to access education. We said yes, and she built it. Today, customers across the country apply for support because one person saw a gap, and a customer decided to fill it. It's now her baby, and no matter what happens in the future, her legacy is baked into VIDA.

Her story reminded us of something we'd seen since the early days of VIDA: our customers have hidden talents and untapped potential. With the right support and opportunity, they don't just show up; they step *into their gifts*. Sandra just took it to another level. We knocked on her door and invited her in with a real role and a belief that she had more gifts to offer than the system had ever allowed her to show.

She wasn't an outlier. She was proof that our platform model was becoming real. VIDA was more than fixing broken buildings. It was about activating potential inside our walls, inside our people. That's what the VIDA platform does: it connects, elevates, and compounds. And it was starting to work.

The next shift in the platform came in how we chose our customers to begin with. As we grew, it became more obvious: the tenant screening process used in the rental industry was completely broken.

* * *

Most large landlords rely on variations of the same shallow and outdated playbook when it comes to screening tenants: they run credit scores and maybe a background check. Some verify employment and other references. It ignores everything that matters: Who someone is. How they live. Their future plans and what they value. The process is wildly out of sync with the realities of people's lives—a system built for efficiency, not understanding. A system in need of a complete overhaul.

Why should a missed phone bill from three years ago stop someone from getting a fresh start? Why is a low credit score treated like a life sentence?

What we really want to know is if you care about your community. Do you take responsibility for your actions? If things get tight, do you go silent or do you reach out? Those are the real signals of financial reliability. That's what we care about: how you live today and how you show up when things get hard.

I had terrible credit growing up. I didn't pay bills on time. That experience stuck with me—how unfair it is that your past can block you from moving forward. That realization landed hard. What really matters? Safety. Security. Empathy. Being a good neighbour. Caring about where you live and who lives next to you. But the traditional rental screening process doesn't look at any of that.

We asked ourselves, *How do you screen for the stuff that actually matters?* I'd seen this play out in my security company. We didn't just want guards who could stand at a post; we wanted people who could serve and protect with empathy and care. We had to look deeper. Same thing here. Cleanliness, for example, is a huge indicator. If someone doesn't care about their space, odds are they won't care about anyone else's either. That impacts the entire building.

So we went back to the drawing board on the entire application process. It was about attracting the right people. Most screen for who someone used to be. We look at who they are today and who they want to become.

This meant making deliberate trade-offs. Frances Frei, in her book *Uncommon Service*, talks about how great companies don't try to be great at everything. They choose where to excel. We did the same. We slowed things down on purpose to go deeper on what *actually matters*: Fit. Values. Community alignment. We added friction in the right places so we could build stronger, more stable communities.

Instead of a quick credit check and a few basic questions, we asked, "Who are you? What's your story? Where are you heading in life?"

Some people look at that and say, "That's none of your business." And that's fine. They self-select out. But others see it as a chance to share something real. In the beginning, that alone helped filter for people who cared.

Over time, we built on this. We added data-driven questions. We ask things like "How important is safety to you?" and "How important is community?" If someone scores low on those, they're probably not a good fit. It's like trying to sell a product to someone who doesn't want it.

We also started sharing a short, honest, up-front "clearing statement" video. It told prospective customers exactly what VIDA is and what it isn't. We said, "If you're looking for brand-new finishes and luxury amenities, this probably isn't for you." These are affordable wood-frame buildings. Sound travels. Kids run around. Dogs bark. If you're not okay with that, you might want to look elsewhere. But if you value community, independence, and affordability, you might feel right at home.

This approach is still one of our best tools for avoiding unnecessary conflict. Before, we only found out after someone moved in that the environment wasn't right for them. By then, it was too late. We had to offer to break their lease, refund their deposit, and help them find a better fit.

So we adjusted. We created a system to determine fit before move-in. It made a huge difference. We also realized this process filtered out no-shows—people who apply, book a tour, and never show up. In our industry, that happens about 30% of the time. But after we introduced this deeper application process, our no-show rate dropped to under 5%.

It was about attracting people who care. When someone takes 10 minutes to fill out thoughtful answers and watches a video about our pillars, they're already showing a level of commitment that goes way beyond ticking boxes.

Then we got even smarter. My cousin Matt, a CFA student at the time, joined VIDA on a short work term to help us analyze our early application data. We asked him to find patterns. What kind of answers were linked to good or bad tenancy outcomes? And Matt found gold.

His first finding: last-minute applicants had an 85% default rate. If someone applied last-minute—for example, on a Thursday hoping to move in by Monday—there was an 85% chance they would default on rent. We inferred they were being evicted and scrambling to find a new place. In some cases, this was a massive red flag. On the flip side, applicants who applied weeks or months in advance were much more stable. These weren't opinions; they were patterns. And we used them to build a better screening system.

The second insight was about smoking. Smokers had a higher default rate. They were more likely to prioritize their smoking addiction over rent and more likely to break rules by smoking indoors in the winter. That created complaints, friction, and community tension.

Those insights helped us build scoring metrics—not to disqualify people but to dig deeper where needed. The application process became smarter, more targeted, and more protective of the communities we were building.

Today, our customer screening process is in a league of its own. It's AI-supported and data-backed, and it takes a human-centred approach. We even have our own in-house data scientist who owns the process, something virtually unheard of in this industry. But at VIDA, it's essential. The result is stronger communities. Lower default rates. Longer tenancies. And a much better way to bring in the right people, who will enjoy their experience, from the start.

That shift redefined everything—not just how we house people but how we build trust, surface talent, and create opportunity.

Then it hit me: how could we screen to find more Sandras?

* * *

The traditional property manager model never made it into the 21st century. It's archaic, overbuilt, and untouched by innovation. I always say roles like that come with an expiry date. When your phone's ringing 24/7, burnout isn't a risk. It's a guarantee.

I had an early idea for a decentralized approach to property management like what we did with security coordinators in the security company.

I started thinking, *Why can't we do the same thing here?*

What if, instead of full-time salaries and always-on-call supers, we had customers managing 12 to 50 units part time while holding other jobs? It was a modern twist on the traditional superintendent model. The old setup often had one person managing up to 200 units—a role built for burnout and totally out of sync with how people live and work today.

My vision was different: built for balance, decentralized, and aligned with the modern realities of flexible work, side hustles, and shared responsibility. It would be a side hustle that added value to their lives without requiring them to leave their building. They'd earn rent credits and learn new skills, but more importantly, they'd help build a sense of community.

They'd run events, onboard new customers, help with showings, distribute notices, help collect rent, coordinate with contractors, and manage issues. It was more about community leadership than property maintenance.

Our philosophy: more people doing less. It's efficient, it's sustainable, and it delivers better service. Think low cost, high touch. That's the VIDA model.

What started as a rethink of how we choose customers was about to expand into every corner of the business. From whom we hired to how we scaled, the platform was waking up, and it needed systems. That included how we identified future leaders within our communities—customers ready to take ownership, contribute, and help us scale the model from the inside out. We used the same lens we had developed for customer screening: alignment, values, empathy, follow-through. Not titles or credentials.

We started asking different questions: Did they care about where they lived? Were they natural problem-solvers? When things went wrong, did they take the initiative or wait for someone else?

We weren't looking for perfect people. We were looking for people who gave a damn. People who took pride in their space. Because if they took pride in their own unit, they'd take pride in the building. And if they didn't? You could feel it the second you walked in.

I remember visiting a building in the early days to meet one of our superintendents at their unit. The second I stepped inside I knew. Dishes piled in the sink, clothes everywhere, the musty smell of damp air and stale food. Takeout containers galore. It looked like a frat house after a weekend bender. That was the lightbulb moment: pride isn't just about how you work. It's how you live.

But how do you screen for that?

We needed something better than an interview. Something that cut through the fluff. I took inspiration from what Southwest Airlines asked their frontline staff: Are you willing to work overtime? Say no and you're done. No second chances.

So we created our own knockout rule: we don't hire a superintendent until we've seen their home, either in person or virtually.

Why? Because if someone doesn't take care of their own space, they're not going to take care of a building. But if their place is clean and organized, that usually means they'll bring that same care to their community. It's simple, and it works.

That knockout became one of our best tools. It filtered out the wrong candidates early and saved us time, money, and future headaches. We weren't looking for people to fill a role. We were looking for leaders in the community. And we started finding them.

Just like with our customer screening process, it wasn't perfect. But we learned fast. We added filters, structured questions, and clearer expectations. The goal wasn't to create a new hierarchy. It was to activate the people already embedded in the community. People who could be a bridge between VIDA and their neighbours. People who would own their role in shaping the place they called home.

By this point we'd learned enough about language upgrades that we knew *superintendent* had to go. We needed something that spoke to leadership, empowerment, and connection.

Building Ambassador.

Leader. Connector. Neighbour.

Sure enough, the answer was right there behind every door the whole time. We just needed to knock.

And it all started with a smile in a hallway.

CHAPTER 6

Scaling Trust from the Ground Up

LET'S BE CLEAR: THE ONLY WAY TO TRULY REVOLU-tionize affordable housing was to crack the code on something no one else had figured out: how to deliver high-touch customer service at radically low cost. We wanted to be the Southwest Airlines or Toyota of housing: operationally lean, relentlessly customer-focused, and built on trust. But unlike airlines or car companies, we weren't just dealing with brand loyalty. We were up against decades of broken trust between landlords and tenants.

We had to prove that low cost didn't have to mean low customer service. That you could scale human connection without bloated overhead. And that rebuilding trust wasn't only possible; it was the foundation that fuelled everything.

When I first started testing the idea of Building Ambassadors, I didn't have it all figured out. It was just a vision—neighbours helping neighbours, people who were invested in their community because they lived there too. But turning that vision into something real was a whole different challenge.

That was when Kyla entered the picture.

She moved into one of our buildings in Halifax in 2018, before the BA role even had a name. She, her brother, Alex, and their dog, Baxter, had been looking for a place that was both affordable and pet-friendly. That was when they found VIDA. What they didn't realize at the time was that they were stepping into the early stages of something much bigger.

One day, I got a call from her that I'll never forget. She didn't sugarcoat anything. "I've got to tell you," she said, "this VIDA thing sounds interesting, but you guys are some of the worst communicators I've ever seen. I don't even know who to talk to about renewing a lease, and I just found out you ran a community contest that's already over. I feel completely out of the loop."

She was blunt. And she was right. We didn't yet have the systems worked out. But instead of getting defensive, I did what I always do: I leaned into the problem and looked for the opportunity. Just like the customer tossing diapers out the window who became a BA, I saw a clue, not a complaint. After hearing her out, I asked, "Would you be interested in becoming a Building Ambassador?"

I explained the model: a part-time leader, someone the community could go to for answers, connection, and support. Someone who already had a full-time job but wanted to make an impact right where they lived. Luckily for us, yes was the answer. And just like that, the BA model started to take shape.

Kyla's raw feedback made it painfully clear: we were dropping the ball on communication, and it was costing us. We weren't just stepping into buildings. We were stepping into years of frustration, neglect, and broken promises. That kind of baggage doesn't fade fast. Rebuilding trust in spaces where it's been eroded for so long is a full-on uphill climb.

And onward and upward the model went because people like Kyla kept showing us what was possible.

* * *

What took me years to learn in the security company was simple but brutal: you can't scale ambition without structure. We had passion. We had purpose. But we were bleeding money and burning out good people. Everything changed when we cracked the model: cut midlevel management, empowered frontline leaders, and built tight, scalable systems. I wasn't going to make that mistake twice.

And Kyla helped show the way. She worked full time in childcare and had a natural talent for bringing order to chaos. One of the first things she did was solve a pest issue no one else had cracked. Instead of waiting on third-party contractors, she rolled up her sleeves, went to local supply stores, and asked for advice. Armed with steel wool, spray foam, and determination, she found the holes and sealed them up. The mice disappeared.

That would have been impressive enough, but she didn't stop there. She educated her customers, left behind tips, and turned a complaint into a moment of connection.

Her impact went far beyond pest control. She did more than just take on the role. She helped define it. She planted gardens that turned a drab exterior into something people felt proud of. And when kids were tearing through the halls and tensions were rising during the pandemic, she created a playroom. A space just for them. The noise stopped. Parents exhaled. The kids had a blast. And she did it all with no direction from leadership. She just saw the need and took the bull by the horns.

Kyla was already doing the role we called Community Leader. Her out-of-the-box thinking didn't just solve problems. It redefined what community care could look like.

She became what we now call an OG. One of the first customers to help shape the BA model into something real. Her journey from frustrated customer to trusted leader proved what this platform was built to do: not just fix buildings but help people step into their gifts and build communities of belonging.

It's one my favourite examples of what happens when you believe in the potential of your customers in an industry that wasn't built for that kind of thinking.

Everything was built around leases, rules, and restrictions, not service and collaboration. Even the Residential Tenancy Board, the closest thing to a regulatory standard, had nothing to say about experience or expectations. It was all, "Here's what you can't do." Nothing that said, "You're a customer, and you deserve better."

That gap became crystal clear after I had the privilege to speak at a customer service conference in Cleveland hosted by John DiJulius, one of the leading minds in the space. He's the guy who helped Starbucks overhaul their customer experience by introducing something called a Customer Bill of Rights. It was a brilliant flip: don't just tell people what they can't do; tell them what they can expect. Be solutions-focused. Be human.

That stuck with me.

Back in the security company, we had created something similar: a Customer Bill of Rights that laid out our promises. Response within 48 hours. Clear expectations. No fine print or passive-aggressive signs. No hiding behind policy.

We brought that thinking to VIDA.

We were at the forefront of a shift in affordable housings, treating tenants like customers. So creating a Customer Bill of Rights was the natural next step. And it became a fundamental part of our model.

VIDA's Customer Bill of Rights outlines what people can count on: timely responses, clean and safe homes, and access to community events and perks. We train for it. We onboard with it. We live it.

And we measure it with customer satisfaction surveys. We ask questions tied to our pillars and our brand promises. It helps us measure where we're doing well and where we need to improve. It keeps us honest and holds us accountable.

Today, every new customer receives our Customer Bill of Rights in their onboarding package, and we post it at the entrance of every building, in plain sight. No fine print. No guesswork. Just a clear promise of what they can count on.

The model was building momentum. We had our pillars. Our Customer Bill of Rights. Our BA model and Community Contractor programs were taking shape. We had communication rhythms and a system to support them.

But something was missing.

How could we actually create a sense of belonging?

And the answer to that question led us down an unexpected path. Not through policy or playbooks but through something far more human.

* * *

In communities where people often live past 100, known as Blue Zones, one factor shows up over and over: a deep sense of belonging. People live longer not just because of diet or exercise but because they feel seen, valued, and connected.

I wondered, *What if our buildings could spark that kind of connection? What if our spaces could make people feel like they mattered, just by showing up differently?*

One weekend, I was at the Discovery Centre in Halifax with my kids, our usual Saturday outing. While they were obsessing over toys, I was scanning the shelves, looking for something a little more...me.

That was when I spotted a book called *Joyful.* The cover popped. And I thought, *Finally something different from the usual "fix yourself" business books.* I picked it up and started flipping through, and within a few pages, I was hooked.

The book talks about how colour, sound, shapes, and physical environments impact mental health way more than we think. One case study was about how painting murals in New York neighbourhoods reduced crime rates. In Europe, colourful buildings lifted spirits. I was sitting there thinking, *Oh my god, this is it.*

I remembered the bright doors of Dublin. And those famously colourful houses in St. John's, Newfoundland. I used to think they were just creative towns. Turns out, they were practical. Fog was so thick that fishermen painted their homes in bold colours to find their way back. Not just beautiful. Functional.

That was when the concept of VIDA-fication really clicked into place: a process of bringing new life to older buildings, making them feel warm, inviting, and full of pride. It was about creating functional belonging.

Sometimes that meant security upgrades, new light fixtures, fresh common areas, or fencing in a patch of grass so it could become a place to gather or a dog park. We got creative, finding room for mini gyms, library nooks, or shared spaces that helped turn buildings into communities.

It also meant bold paint and bright doors.

We picked 12 Lego-bright colours and piloted the concept in one of our buildings. We painted the doors red, yellow, blue, and green and then launched a community contest where customers could name their doors. Suddenly, it wasn't "I live in Unit 12." It was "I live in the bright robin's-egg blue on the third floor."

People weren't just customers anymore. They were neighbours. They had pride. Identity.

But not everyone agreed on the colours. Cue the great paint debate.

Natalie, my wife, who's an incredible interior designer, wanted muted, sophisticated tones—think warm neutrals and soft palettes. I wanted colour that punched you in the face in the best way possible. Bold, bright, unapologetic. Colour that said, "Someone gives a damn here." It was less of a design debate and more of a cold war with paint swatches. Tensions were high. Opinions were stronger. And no one was backing down.

We didn't talk for two weeks.

I decided to settle it the only way I knew how: with a test. We picked two neighbouring buildings and painted some doors in Natalie's designer tones and others in my vibrant, kid-with-a-crayon-box shades. Then we asked customers which ones they liked better.

Kid-in-a-crayon-box won.

Natalie was gracious, but I still joke that that door exercise nearly got me evicted!

We still do VIDA-fication today, but in a world of rising costs and inflation, we've had to get sharper about what's a must-have versus a nice-to-have. But we've learned that when you show up and create spaces of belonging, whether that's a painted door, community garden, or playroom, pride and belonging follow.

But pride and belonging don't just come from what you add—they come from how you respond when trust is tested.

Take a pest issue we had in one of our Halifax communities. One customer was beyond frustrated, and the frontline team got defensive about why it hadn't been resolved. I pulled everyone into the lobby of the impacted building and said, "We're not here to argue sides or figure out who's right or wrong. We're here to figure out what we missed—and how we can be better."

Because behind every tough conversation is an underlying lesson. And a chance to build trust.

At VIDA, leadership means spending the time to figure out what that lesson is. It means looking in the mirror and getting to the right questions: Did we communicate clearly, act fast enough? Did we uphold our Customer Bill of Rights, our pillars?

That same sense of responsibility drives bold moves too—but they don't always land well with everyone.

We once invested $10,000 of personal money in a massive mural on the side of one of our buildings, not from a capital plan, not for optics. We didn't have to do it. But we felt a responsibility to show that this place matters. Our customers matter. The intent was to paint a vision of what the community could become.

In fact, that mural is on the cover of this book—a reminder that real change starts with seeing potential and investing in the people who call it home.

As you'd expect, not everyone got it. Some loved it. Others asked, "Why are you spending money on a mural when I want new floors?"

We'll never satisfy every customer—or every comment

thread. We're here to keep communities clean, safe, and affordable. To make intentional moves that build pride and belonging.

And to own our responsibility—*every time*.

* * *

When a home (unit) becomes vacant, customers apply to join VIDA. Others come to us when we acquire their building. In both cases, trust starts at the door. But with acquisitions, we have to earn our way in.

When VIDA takes over a building, customers are rightfully scared. Will rents spike? Will they be evicted? Are we just another landlord in disguise?

That's actually one of the reasons I'm writing this book. Every new VIDA customer, including those in newly acquired buildings, will receive a copy. Our hope is that it helps them understand the mission and feel they're part of it. And if you're a customer reading this, this is more than a story about you. It's a story because of you. Thanks for being part of it.

We all know that talk is cheap. What matters is how you show up. And when it comes to acquisitions, that presence needs to be fast and it needs to be human.

That's why we started holding town halls within 30 days of every acquisition. I'll never forget that first one when only one person showed up. Her name was Janet.

Janet was visibly nervous. She kept her distance, arms crossed, eyes scanning. As we took her through everything VIDA was about—our commitment to keeping rents low and our community perks, events, and opportunities—her facial expressions said it all.

First confusion. Then disbelief. And then tears. She cried

in the middle of the town hall. Blown away, she told us, "I've lived in this building for 15 years and have only met my landlord once."

The next day, we were flooded with messages from other customers. Janet had spread the word. In a game of inches, this moment felt like a mile. And it told us everything.

We realized transparency builds trust faster than any tool. From then on, it became a standard: host a town hall within 30 days of every acquisition. We also introduced quarterly town halls with our BAs to share updates, understand challenges, and celebrate wins.

Alone, they're just actions. But stacked together, they move the needle.

One of my favourite examples of building trust through innovation came in 2020. The space we were in was already fragile. We were acquiring buildings full of people who didn't know us, didn't ask for us, and didn't trust us yet.

Then the pandemic hit.

Customers were scared. Uncertain. This was global chaos crashing into local fear. And we were right in the middle of it.

The model was already bold, already people-first. But even with BAs in place—people on-site who could listen, advocate, and connect—it was an uphill climb. And now it was about to be tested under pressure no one saw coming.

Once it took hold, no one knew what was real. Information was flying in from all directions: social media, the news, word of mouth. It was chaos. No one knew what to believe or what was actually happening.

But as always, within chaos lies huge opportunity. If we could cut through the noise and give people something calm, clear, and consistent, we could win them over when it counted most.

So we launched a daily blast. Every day at 3:00, every customer got a message from us. No fluff. No fear tactics. Just the facts: what was happening with the pandemic, what restrictions were in place, updates from the government, and what it meant for them. Local, specific, clear.

We wanted to be the one voice people could count on when everything else felt shaky. And that was exactly what we became.

As those updates kept coming, something started to shift. People calmed down. The anxiety began to settle. The messages started landing. Some customers told us it was the only thing they relied on. Others said it was the one thing they looked forward to each day.

I knew we had a unique chance to turn fear into connection. To show up for them, especially when everything else felt like it was falling apart. I knew we could take it even further.

Many of our customers were on the front lines—healthcare workers, cleaners, grocery clerks—risking their health just to hold on to a paycheque. Others had already lost their jobs, and the government hadn't rolled out much support at this point. There was no safety net. Just fear, isolation, and uncertainty.

So we shifted gears. We knew people needed more than just information. They were longing for structure. Support. A sense of routine. Small wins to carry them through the day.

We started sharing family-friendly activities to do in isolation: simple and nutritious recipes, mental health tips, and home workouts that didn't require a gym or equipment. Stuff that said, "We see you. You're not alone."

The response was incredible. Customers started writing in, telling us how much it helped, that it gave them something to look forward to. Something that felt normal. Something that made them feel cared for.

I could feel the momentum.

Back when I ran Source Security, we used themes—small contests and morale boosters that kept the energy up. We brought that idea into VIDA.

At the height of the pandemic, as people were forced into self-isolation, we wanted to bring smiles to people's faces. We launched a lip-sync contest. Something light. Something fun. It was free to enter. The only thing it cost was a little courage and a few minutes of joy. The ask was simple: record a lip-sync video, solo or with your family. If we hit 100 submissions across the VIDA community, we'd give away a grand prize of one month's free rent.

We ended up receiving over 200 entries. Everyone got involved. Even our staff joined in and shared videos. It took over our YouTube channel. The media even picked it up.

It made national news: a real estate company not just helping customers financially but supporting their mental health and building real community during a pandemic. It was one of the most powerful examples of what's possible when people come together, even in a crisis.

We turned a tough situation into something meaningful. Something that lifted people up. And yeah, it even landed us a CBC feature, which was worth tens of thousands of dollars in free marketing.

It was a great reminder: you don't have to sit back and let the world dictate the terms. You can step up, get creative, and make something extraordinary happen. We added value during one of the most stressful times in recent history, and people felt it.

But let's be real: it isn't just about the wins. It's about how you handle the hard moments. The missteps. The times you fall short.

Like with Ozue.

It was early days, and we were pouring everything into the portfolio, trying to breathe life into buildings that were falling apart.

One day, a customer in Halifax called me. "The pipe is banging against the wall. It's nonstop. We can't sleep." I sent someone out. They said it was fixed.

Next day, same call. "Still banging. We can't sleep. It's affecting our mental health."

So I sent a third-party contractor, but $2,000 later, it was still banging. Because it was an old building, the pipes expanded and contracted with temperature, and the noise was loud. The customer even sent me videos.

After the failed attempts to find a solution, I lost my cool. Frustrated, I told him, "If you're not happy, you can leave."

I know. Not my finest moment.

In this industry, there's often an unspoken assumption that customers can't be trusted. That they're exaggerating. Complaining. And in that moment, I fell into the same trap. My Irish temper got the best of me, and I didn't show empathy. He had a valid concern. Some situations just call for showing up and owning it in person—so that's what I did.

He opened the door—a big Nigerian guy towering over me.

I smiled. "We almost came to blows on the phone. But I still think I could take you." He burst out laughing.

We sat down, had tea, and talked. I apologized and said, "You weren't treated like a customer. I'm sorry. Let's figure this out."

That conversation changed everything. He later became a BA for the building. He was engaged and reliable, and he brought real value to the community.

Eventually, I was invited to his wedding in Halifax—a beautiful celebration, by the way. I met his family, saw the richness of his culture, and felt honoured to be there.

Today, Ozue runs his own moving company in Halifax. While he is no longer a BA and living at VIDA, he's one of our community partners, helping VIDA customers move in and out. Great service, great price. That's the ripple effect of community. When you trust and invest in people, they reciprocate. Everybody wins.

Those who know me well know I'm not the best at handling heated situations.

That's why today we have Haley Hickey, VIDA's dedicated Customer Concierge. Her job is 100% customer satisfaction. She picks up the phone when most people wouldn't. And she doesn't stop until the customer feels heard, respected, and taken care of.

Still, I worried as we grew. *Am I drifting too far from the customer?* That question kept me up at night. Growth is great, but growth creates distance. And if you're not careful, distance becomes disconnect. So we built a few grounding principles to fight that drift.

Jack Welch has a line I love: "Nothing gets bought or sold at the head office, so why do people spend so much time there?" This was like music to my ears!

At a West Point leadership conference, we heard a phrase that landed just as well: "Taste the pizza." For us, it meant everyone, including finance and admin, getting out of the office. Walk the buildings. Talk to customers. See things for yourself. We turned it into a habit, not just a reaction when things went wrong.

We added another accountability layer: senior BA backup. If a customer had an issue reaching their BA, they now had a second point of contact. Someone else they could go to within to community. Simple. Effective.

This approach helps us stay closer to our customers. It's the *moments* like this that help keep me energized.

Janet reminded us what it means to see the human behind the acquisition—not just a unit but a person with history, fear, and hope. Ozue reminded us how important it is to own our mistakes. And the pandemic? That was when we became agents of trust.

None of that happened by accident. It took our team showing up again and again, doing the hard work.

And when you do that enough times, you can't help but start thinking bigger.

* * *

VIDA started with a few buildings and a simple idea: treat people like customers, not problems. But soon we were doing much more than turning around properties. We were building trust, restoring pride, and laying the foundation for a new kind of housing company. A platform. A movement.

Kyla's story isn't a one-off. Neither is Ozue's. Or Janet's. They're part of a growing segment of Canada's working class, caught between rising costs and shrinking options. Overlooked. Let down by the very systems meant to support them. Some call it the missing middle. That's the gap VIDA was built to fill.

We rebuilt the system to serve them and then watched *them* transform it. They started out as Building Ambassadors—leaders, connectors, people with pride in their communities. But over time they became something more.

They became *Ambassadors of Belonging.*

And I couldn't be prouder.

We've seen BAs and customers who've bought their first

cars, taken their first vacations, even purchased their first homes. At the time of writing this, I learned that a customer gave their BA a car. Not a thank-you card. Not a gift card. A car!

There are countless more stories like that unfolding quietly in our communities every day. Moments of generosity, growth, and trust that no system can force but the right platform can make possible.

Once VIDA reached 500 units, the calls got louder. The opportunities came faster. That shift forced a question—not about *what* we were doing but about *how far* we were willing to go.

It was one of those moments where you either walk away or double down.

I chose to double down.

But that meant saying no to everything I was involved in that didn't serve VIDA's mission. And like I always do when the stakes are high, I wrote. I needed something to meet the moment.

I came up with VIDA's Big Hairy Audacious Goal (BHAG): 10,000 units by 2027.

That was it. That was the line in the sand.

But a bold goal is useless without a way to make it real. You can't hire your way out of every problem. To build something like VIDA, you need systems that turn customers into leaders and grow people, not just payroll.

As VIDA grew, so did the complexity. And like one of our advisors, Verne Harnish, says, "As companies scale, they naturally add complexity. The real power comes in simplifying as you grow."

That was where the true power of decentralization came in.

CHAPTER 7

Outrageous Empowerment

WHEN I PLANTED OUR FIRST BHAG, I SET A STAKE IN the ground: 10,000 units by 2027. I did the math, and that could easily be a global brand. The idea of creating that kind of impact got me fired up. Could I actually do this? Could we really transform housing at that scale?

Of course I started telling people, which is what I do to put pressure on myself to bring big visions or decisions to life. Some told me, "You might want to keep that to yourself." But I couldn't. Talking about it made it real. And the more skepticism I got, the more driven I became.

Still, with my passion for building world-class teams and culture, I thought, *We've got this.* But to actually deliver, I had to cut all the noise. Focus. So I let go of everything else. VIDA wasn't just another business. It was a way to change lives at scale.

On an afternoon walk came the conversation with my wife, Natalie. She asked the question that mattered most: could I do this without sacrificing the people I love?

Something always gets sacrificed when you're building

something big, and too often, it's family. I've seen it happen: the guy accepting an award, thanking his wife for raising the kids and holding everything together. I'll never give that speech. To me, that's not partnership. It's absence disguised as ambition.

I know what it feels like to have a dad who isn't around. I won't repeat that pattern. If this ever costs me the chance to be truly present with my family—Georgia, Wellington, Margot—or to show up for my commitments to community, boards, or mentorship, I'll walk away. No mission, no number, no unit count is worth losing what matters most.

I've met plenty of people who built empires but lost their kids, their marriages, their peace. I kept wondering, *Why can't I crack that code? Why does success always seem to come at that kind of price?*

That afternoon walk with Natalie reminded me what could get lost in the pursuit of a dream. That's the line I carry with me now. If we're building something great, it has to include the people we love. Otherwise, what's the point?

That commitment runs deep in VIDA.

* * *

From day one, innovation shaped VIDA's story, but it was focus that turned our Big Hairy Audacious Goals into real progress.

We didn't stumble into focus. We built it deal by deal, decision by decision. We made hard calls early: cut what didn't fit and doubled down on what did. The model had to do more than just scale; it needed to get better at what made it work in the first place.

The VIDA brand needed to evolve as well.

Back then, we were called VIDA Living. Aqua-coloured logo, good vibes, clean design. It looked fine. But it didn't feel like us anymore. We were growing up, and the brand wasn't.

So I called Phil, a close friend and branding expert with instincts sharp enough to gut-check your whole identity before you've finished your pitch.

He asked the big question. "Ron, I love what you're building, but are you chasing local vibes or planning on building something that stands shoulder to shoulder with Amazon, Amex, and Apple?"

"Global. No question."

"Then lose the training wheels. Drop 'Living.' It's just VIDA."

It hit like a gut punch. But I've learned to sit in that discomfort because that's where the truth lives. I always say it: if I'm not uncomfortable, I'm bored. And those moments of discomfort have led to our biggest breakthroughs. He was right. The word wasn't adding anything. *VIDA* stood stronger on its own.

So we dropped it. No more *Living*.

Just VIDA.

Simple. Bold. Focused.

That same instinct—shed what doesn't fit—started becoming my strongest filter.

I still owned about 50,000 square feet across three commercial buildings. On paper, this made sense: a diversified portfolio that was a long-term wealth strategy for my family. But they didn't align with VIDA's mission or any of the values we were building around. I kept thinking about something Verne Harnish had said: "If you want to build a unicorn, you need the courage to be laser focused."

I made the call to sell all my commercial holdings—even the

milestone building I bought at 29 for $1.75 million. At that point, it felt like everything. But the things that give you oxygen early on can start to suffocate you later if you're not paying attention.

Those assets had served their purpose. Selling them was the clearest signal I could send to myself and to my team that I was all in on VIDA (I also happened to sell just before the COVID-19 pandemic, which was some of the best market timing of my life).

But focus alone wouldn't get us to 10,000 units. We needed systems that could support a decentralized model, stay flexible for innovation, and still keep us grounded in what mattered most.

That was when I came across Jim Collins's *Turning the Flywheel*. It was only 35 pages, but it hit hard. The idea was simple: your business is a wheel. It's about creating momentum by aligning the right levers in your business. When everything works together, the flywheel spins faster. But if even one piece is off, the whole thing slows down.

Mastering the flywheel, Collins said, is what separates good companies from great ones. Think Amazon-level success.

Each metric has subcomponents, and if even one scores below an 8 out of 10, that part needs fixing. Simple. Brutal. Effective. It gave us the perfect bridge between purpose and pressure, a way to chase big goals without losing sight of why we started.

At VIDA, our flywheel had to do one thing: keep us laser focused on revolutionizing affordable communities. Every part of it—acquiring workforce housing, VIDA-fying the buildings, generating excitement and measuring impact, achieving operational excellence and financial targets, and leveraging VIDA's value growth—had to feed that mission.

So we adopted it.

Now everything we do runs through the same filter: does it make the flywheel spin faster?

This not only provides our team lots to debate when it comes to decision-making but gives us the incredible gift of discipline. Every system we build, every decision we make, is about one thing: creating momentum that can sustain itself.

The flywheel had started to spin. Now we had to keep it going.

* * *

Before VIDA, I learned what happens when you remove middle management and bet on the front lines.

In my last company, Source Security, we did just that. We blew up the org chart. Stripped out the layers of control. Empowered the people closest to the action and gave them the tools to make smart calls in real time.

It wasn't theory.

It was how we saved the company.

We were on the edge. Burnout, chaos, zero margin. Removing middle management didn't just cut costs. It changed everything. We unlocked speed, ownership, accountability, and pride. We cleared bottlenecks. People started making better decisions faster. And it changed the culture overnight.

I knew then what most people still don't: if you empower the front lines, you will solve most of your issues. That shift became the blueprint. And at VIDA, we ran with it.

Whenever I talk about our decentralized model—running nearly 3,000 units across four provinces—people in real estate look at me like I'm speaking another language. Some even roll their eyes. "No property manager? No leasing agent?"

When I say, "We don't have either," they think I'm joking.

But it's true. VIDA has no property managers. No leasing agents. No midlevel management. In fact, not a single person on our team comes from real estate.

We just have a decentralized model built around Building Ambassadors who live where they lead, Community Leaders who are seasoned BAs turned mentors, the Building Services Team (BST) who are pros in repairs and maintenance and also help train customers, and Community Contractors who pitch in on light repairs, landscaping, and more.

Today, VIDA is the only landlord in North America saving up to 40% on select operating costs by redirecting work away from third parties and into the hands of our own residents. That kind of savings didn't happen by accident. It came from pressure—runaway inflation, soaring interest rates, tightening rent controls.

It did more than test our resilience. It pushed us to evolve. Our decentralized model sharpened into something stronger: team-based leadership (more on that in the next chapter).

But if you want to understand how a strong model gets built, start with the moments where it began to bend. For us, that moment started with a phone call.

Back in 2018–2019, we had just finished heavy renovations on our first 100 units. Most of them had been stripped to the studs. I had originally imagined buying buildings with existing customers, but in this case, we had construction crews on-site, and we were renting out units as we stabilized them. But things still went wrong—constantly. We had a small team of about four people handling repairs and maintenance.

This was early, and the model was still unproven. We were figuring it out in real time. One day, our head of repairs called me. He came from an old-school command-and-control background, and he didn't hold back.

"This decentralized model? It's not going to fly," he said. "You can't just hand people autonomy and expect it to work. They need to call someone like me who has the experience. And we need three more people on the repair team. We're drowning."

I remember thinking more people just meant less opportunity to find solutions in the community. We didn't need people to manage problems. We needed people to teach our BAs and train customers how to solve them. In fact, we needed to cut the four we already had. The numbers just didn't work. Major renovations were wrapping up. We needed a better way.

So I did what I always do when something breaks down: I went straight to the bottleneck. I told him, "No problem. For the next two weeks, I'm the repair and maintenance team. You focus on your stuff. I'll take every call."

I told the BAs, "Call me if you need anything." What most people don't know is that I'm terrible with tools. I can barely use a screwdriver. But that made me perfect for the job. I wasn't going to fix anything. I was going to fix the root problem.

Steve Jobs used to say he'd sit in the problem until it spoke to him. That was what I was doing. I wanted to feel the friction firsthand—to live it, not just lead through it.

Then the calls started coming in from BAs. "Hey, the power's out in half the unit. I'm trying to figure out what's going on."

I'd ask, "What do you think you should do?"

They'd pause. "Maybe I could try resetting the breaker. It's probably just tripped."

"Awesome," I'd say. "Try it. Let me know how it goes. And if it works, take a video so we can share it."

Next call, same thing.

"There's a bit of water pooling under the kitchen sink. I think the pipe's leaking."

I'd ask, "What do you think you should do?"

And like clockwork, I'd get a potential solution. "I could check if it's the drain trap and tighten it first, then see if it's still leaking before calling anyone."

"Perfect. Give it a shot. Let me know what happens."

By day four, the calls stopped. Not because we had solved everything but because they realized *they* could. I wasn't giving solutions. I was just asking the right questions: What do you think you should do? Why that? Any other ideas?

The old repair team did everything, from leaky taps to full renos. It slowed us down and drove up costs fast. Light repairs moved to BAs and Community Contractors. We later created the BST to handle the heavier jobs and to train BAs and CCs along the way. It gave us a model that was lean, decentralized, and scalable.

And it changed the culture. People used their judgment, learned through experience, and grew stronger with every problem solved. Ownership had moved to the front lines, and we weren't going back.

* * *

Decentralization is the foundation of VIDA's operating model. We used it in security, and we're using it here. But it's not easy. Most companies start decentralized and get more bureaucratic as they grow. They build layers of management. They lose agility. As Jim Collins puts it, you're either nimble with chaos, or you're sluggish with control. Most choose control.

But if you want to scale decentralization, you need balance. Flexibility. What do you let frontliners decide?

When I was building the security company, I kept coming back to one question: how do you actually empower people, not just in theory but in practice? I realized a single decision-making shift changed everything. It was such a turning point that it inspired the subtitle of my first book, *Outrageous Empowerment: The Incredible Story of Giving Employees Their Brains Back.*

Some found the phrase provocative. "Are you saying they didn't have brains to begin with?" No, not at all, but the reality is that most industries create policies and procedures that slowly cook people's brains—layers of policy, approvals, and micromanagement that strip away any sense of pride, innovation, and ownership.

That framework became a springboard for real empowerment—a clear decision-making process with fewer bottlenecks and trust baked into the model. Naturally, I wanted to bring that same approach into VIDA.

In the past, our decision-making framework was simple. If someone was about to do something they hadn't been trained on or didn't have direct experience with, they'd ask themselves three questions. Is it the right thing for the customer? Does it align with our purpose and values? Are you willing to be accountable for your decision?

If the answer to all three is yes, the decision can be made. No approval needed. Move now!

It worked well in the security world. But here, it needed a tweak. I realized, "We need to adjust the first question." In this business, what's right for an individual customer, like throwing a massive party, might not be right for the community. So we changed it. The first question became, Is it the right thing for the community? The other two stayed the same.

I'll never forget Amy, one of our first BAs to put it in action. A customer had reported a bug. Concerned it might be a bedbug, Amy called pest control. It wasn't a bedbug, but we still got a bill for $85. Our head of repairs didn't waste a second. "I told you!" he said. "This can't scale. That BA should've called me. I would've made the decision." He wanted everything to go through him—a typical bottleneck.

But I laughed. "She did exactly what we asked her to do." Amy, the BA, followed the framework. I gave her a $50 gift card after a quick debrief and celebrated her decision.

She told me, "I called pest control because I thought it was the right thing for the community. I didn't want the problem to spread. I believed it was bedbugs, and based on our purpose to revolutionize affordable communities, I thought it was the right call, and I'm willing to own that."

Perfect answer. We celebrated her publicly and used it as a learning moment. We brought in the pest control company to one of our monthly meetings. They walked the team through pest identification—bedbugs versus beetles, what to look for, how to assess. Now when our BAs call pest control, it's because they know it's truly necessary. This is the type of system we are building and an example of an early win: decentralized decision-making. It was a home run.

People always ask me, "Is it working?"

"Absolutely," I say. The framework promotes critical thinking across the company. It's a pre-decision tool.

Leaders can ask, "Before you make a decision, have you walked through the process? If yes, walk me through each question and how you answered it based on this specific situation." It's also a post-coaching tool. This tool is extremely important to scale decision-making in a decentralized environment. It's most commonly used in situations where our team is dealing with an issue they either haven't been trained in or have no previous experience dealing with.

Most frontliners make better decisions than people at the top. They're closer to the issue and closer to the customer, and they see things others don't. About 80% of the time, their decisions are fantastic, and those become the new standard. When that happens, we stop, celebrate, and share the story company-wide. The other 20% become training opportunities, like in the previous pest issue.

And that's the point. We prioritize progress *over* perfection. When someone missteps, it's not a failure. It's a chance to learn, get better, and move forward with more clarity.

And sometimes it reveals a hole in our process—not a people problem but a system one. We learn from the moment. It's one way the model gets sharper over time.

As the model evolved, so did the opportunities. BAs who consistently showed strong judgment, initiative, and leadership weren't just left to plateau. They had a path forward. We called it the Community Leader role: seasoned BAs who could mentor others and strengthen the culture of decentralized leadership from within.

But growth can't rely on instinct alone. As the model expanded, structure had to catch up. Great instincts need support. VIDA needed to do more than empower people. We needed to equip them. That meant figuring out where autonomy belonged and where structure was essential.

Accounts receivable is a good example. We centralized it. When we needed someone to run it, we did what we always do: we looked inside the community first. And sure enough, we found Akhil—a VIDA customer with a background at Amazon.

If someone in Unit 12 isn't picking up the phone, he doesn't sit on it. He messages the BA: "Can you knock and ask them to give me a call?" And if the customer isn't home, no problem. The BA leaves one of our custom-designed door hangers: bright, simple, and unmistakably VIDA. It's a visual nudge that says, "Hey, someone's trying to help. Give us a shout." No shaming. No stress. Just a human nudge.

It's collaborative and efficient, something traditional property managers can't replicate at scale. Because we've got one BA in every building, we don't wait on emails or property managers to act. We move lightning fast. The system is centralized, but the execution is *hyperlocal*. That's what gives us an edge—and speed is just the start.

On the flip side, we decentralized supply ordering. BAs can order cleaning supplies directly through Amazon Business or other channels using pre-vetted low-cost supply lists. They don't need permission. They just use the systems we've built. It's autonomy with support.

That's the magic: balancing accountability, autonomy, and training. Most consultants tell you to centralize. I disagree. Decentralization takes more work to build, but it pays off. It drives buy-in. It builds culture.

In our world, it's not just a competitive advantage. It's a barrier to entry.

That was the next phase of the work: building systems that could help the model scale without softening its edge. Not by adding layers of control but by creating the right scaffolding to let decentralized leadership thrive.

* * *

Decentralization doesn't mean no systems. It means the right systems that empower people, rather than control them.

As we built out our decentralized model, we knew it couldn't stand on its own. We had to create the right support mechanisms to make it work. Drawing on what we'd learned from the security business, we started designing two foundational systems: the Building Ambassador Zone and VIDA University, or VIDA U.

The Building Ambassador Zone includes all our tools, systems, checklists, and documentation. It's where BAs can access what they need to operate: how to build relationships with customers or handle a move-in or unit turnover. VIDA U provides the learning, and the BA Zone houses the execution.

To build the BA Zone, I turned to someone who knew decentralization inside and out: Jodi Tanner, our head of people and culture. Jodi's been with me for over 10 years and is now a partner in the business. She helped build the decentralized systems in the security company, including the Security Coordinator Zone. At VIDA, she took those lessons even further, helping design a next-level system that didn't just support frontliners but empowered them to lead.

VIDA U, our learning management system, was designed specifically for Building Ambassadors. The goal is to help them manage their responsibilities without overwhelming them. Early on, our approach was like drinking from a fire hose. We dumped everything on them at once and expected them to absorb it all. It didn't work.

Jaclyn Saunders, who leads learning and development, stepped in and helped us rethink the system. She brought a critical insight. The science of learning is clear: volume and sequence matter. Flood someone with too much information too fast, and overload kicks in. Worse, not every module is immediately relevant. If a BA doesn't have a move-out in their first month, why force them to memorize the unit turnover process on day one?

Today, VIDA U is more like a "choose your own adventure." BAs start with the essentials—what they'd need if they were handed the keys today—and build from there at their own pace. We focus first on critical foundations: understanding their support network, handling repair and maintenance requests, learning customer service basics, and getting to know their building. The rest, like unit turnovers, comes later, when they actually need it.

It's not just passive learning either. In some modules, they're prompted to take real-world action.

For example, when they hit the module about learning where the water shutoff is in their building, the system tells them to pause the lesson and go physically walk the building. Then they return to the module and continue learning. That integration of knowledge and real-world application is what makes it stand out.

But training only matters if it moves the needle.

From the start, we linked two metrics that mattered most to these systems: customer service and building performance. We introduced net operating income (NOI) early on because BAs needed to understand how their actions impacted the financial strength of their building. Over time, we evolved the language to something even more practical: cash flow, the clearest sign of whether a building can stand on its own. If it's not generating positive cash flow, it's not sustainable.

That connection between training and real-world outcomes was intentional. And today, we've taken it a step further. We track impact. Every Building Ambassador's training is connected to real customer feedback. We ask customers about key pillars, like cleanliness and Building Ambassador response times.

By comparing training progress to customer feedback, we can spot patterns. If a BA scored well on a module but customer satisfaction is low, it signals a coaching opportunity. If multiple BAs are struggling in the same area, it tells us we might need to strengthen the training itself. Either way, the goal is the same: making sure every BA has the tools, support, and clarity to succeed.

These two systems constantly evolve. We revisit content, update tools, and make sure everything is relevant and easy to use. They are living systems that grow with the business and evolve alongside our team.

* * *

The idea was already in motion: customers stepping up to help with painting, drywall, and light repairs. What began informally was ready to evolve, backed by real systems that could scale.

We formalized training for Community Contractors (CCs) through a certification pathway and began tracking quality and consistency of work. CCs weren't just pitching in. They were becoming trusted contributors.

And the value was real. A typical contractor might charge $1,000 to paint a one-bedroom. A trained CC could do it for $650. VIDA saved money. The customer earned extra income.

But most importantly, that same customer gained pride and presence in the community. You could feel the shift. They started showing up differently, taking better care of their unit, helping neighbours, setting a new tone. It was real ownership. And pride like that travelled further than we had ever expected.

One customer might say to another, "Hey, I painted your unit." And just like that, a spark is lit. A new connection forms. The new customer, curious and inspired, signs up to become a Community Contractor herself. Her first job is painting the common-area hallway in her own building. That hallway suddenly means more. It becomes a place of transfer, of knowledge, of ownership, of pride. It's how customers start to see themselves not just as residents but as co-stakeholders—people who shape the community they live in.

And when customers start to see themselves as co-stakeholders, the impact goes beyond the building.

Take Brandi. She moved into VIDA's community as a single mom, starting over and terrified. Brandi stepped up as a Building Ambassador and got busy learning everything from painting to patching potholes. She eventually became a CC. She didn't come in with a resumé full of trade skills. What she had was grit, gifts, and someone willing to bet on her. Today, she's on our BST, training and approving the next wave of Community Contractors.

Sandra's daughter bought her first car with money she earned as a CC. Some customers have used the income to put themselves through school. Others have put their kids through school. Taken their first vacations.

When neglect is the norm, real opportunity feels revolutionary.

And that's the real work of revolutionizing affordable communities: building pride, unlocking potential, and creating new possibilities one customer at a time.

We extended these tasks beyond maintenance at buildings. For smaller projects—bookkeeping, IT, admin work—we looked within our community first. Today, about 20% of our full-time staff started out as customers. They took on small projects, proved themselves, and eventually joined us full time. No different than a large company that looks to their internal team before going to the outside market for new roles. We just apply the strategy to our customers.

That's the power of decentralization done right: blending internal resources with the talent already living in the building. Other companies might hire a resident now and then to shovel snow or sweep a hallway. We built an entire model around it—at scale, with systems and with intention.

And in an industry where property managers often don't even live in the same cities as their buildings, that changes everything. Our people don't just understand the customer. They *are* the customer. They share the hallways. They hear the noise. They feel the wins and frustrations firsthand.

That's what makes this model sustainable. Because it's not some top-down vision being imposed from the outside. It's being shaped, led, and improved on the inside by the very people it was built to serve.

Let me be clear: VIDA's Building Ambassadors run this company. Our job is to support them. The front line is first. Always.

That's why we stopped calling it Head Office. The name never fit. It made it sound like the power lived in some corner office, when it's always been on the ground, with the front line. So we scrapped it and called it what it actually is: the Support Centre. Because that's the job: to back up the people doing the work.

And that's not just a motto. It's how we operate. I tell every new team member if it's 4:00 p.m. on a Friday and you have a missed call from me *and* a BA, you call the BA first. No debate. That's our culture. That's our org chart.

You don't gatekeep. You don't delay. You respond within 24 hours. And yes, we track it. We follow up. Because if the field doesn't feel supported, the whole model breaks.

Testing the BA model in Halifax was just the warm-up.

The real test was coming—in new cities, tougher buildings, and a world tilting into chaos. Could a decentralized, customer-powered model hold up?

We were about to find out.

PART 3

From Bid to Blueprint

CHAPTER 8

The Window into Reality

WE NEEDED MORE CAPITAL. MORE DISCIPLINE. MORE horsepower.

VIDA was growing fast, and I knew the next stage was going to look different. If we really wanted to scale, we'd need to build something that would stand up to institutional partners. Sharper reporting. More structure. And larger transactions.

In the early days of flirting with the idea of raising capital, we didn't have a back office. I was still underwriting most of the deals myself, and I was in over my head. I'd always struggled with numbers, and my dyslexia made it even harder. I thought maybe I should take an accounting course. But I knew one thing for sure: I needed help.

Then I thought of Eric McPherson. Eric is the definition of a "lead from behind" leader. He pushes people forward with calm encouragement: "Let's go. We've got this."

Eric had done some accounting and analysis work for me before moving on to a full-time accounting role with another group, but something had stuck. He was good at accounting, but he was *exceptional* at performing analysis and solving complex problems in a calm way. He had a CFA and a sharp mind. I knew he was what VIDA needed.

"Eric, I need you to come back, but not as an accountant."

"What do you mean?" he asked.

"I know you've done accounting for me before, but I think your real passion is analysis. I need someone who can help us make mature investment decisions. Someone who can speak the language of lenders, dissect deals, and make calls that stand up under pressure. I think this is your calling. I'm building something big, and I want you to be part of it."

He took a few days to think. Then he called me back.

"I'm in," he said. "Let's go!"

In the early days, I started meeting with family offices and investors. Eric wasn't officially the CIO yet. He was just the guy who knew the numbers. But on these calls, people saw him and asked, "Who's that?" So I started introducing him as our chief investment officer. The title stuck.

When I met with family offices, I had a routine. I started by saying, "Nice to meet you. Before I get into what VIDA is all about, I want to ask a few quick questions. Let's assume you like and trust me. Let's assume you believe in VIDA—our platform, our mission. And let's assume you like the deal we're putting in front of you. Now, one: how much are you comfortable investing in a single deal? Two: could you invest more before your capital was recycled through refinancing or sale?"

In the early days, I heard, "If we like everything, we could probably do $500,000" or "Maybe $1 million." Some said $5 million.

And I said, "Thanks for your time, but I think we're not the right fit. We're going to scale quickly, and we'll outgrow you too fast."

Eric's jaw dropped every time. "They're ready to write a cheque!" he said.

"We need partners who see the big picture and have lots of liquidity," I told him. "It's better to hear no a few times now than to waste time with smaller, short-term capital partners."

That strategy paid off. It let us stay focused and find the right long-term investors. Like when I was introduced to Mike Foy.

Mike is the kind of guy you don't forget. Bear presence. Football build. Brain like a Wall Street banker. He played for what some call the Notre Dame of Canada. Reads constantly. Always thinking 10 steps ahead. The first time I met him, I thought, *This guy's already seen the moves I haven't even thought of yet.*

I told him about our model. Our vision. Our future growth plans. He listened. Then he leaned back and hit me with two questions that stopped me in my tracks.

"Ron, you bought that deal in Winnipeg at a discount because it was a tough asset. But those don't come in bulk. How are you going to get to 10,000 units doing one-off deals like that?"

I opened my mouth to respond, but I had nothing.

Then came the second question: "You talk about chaos—stabbings, kicked-in windows, unpredictable tenants. You love systems. But how do you systemize chaos? How do you scale when you can't predict what's next?"

That one landed hard.

Up to that point in the early days, I believed we could. We'd just proven that decentralization could work. That Building Ambassadors could lead with clarity and autonomy. That customers could step up and take ownership.

But Mike's question exposed a critical blind spot: we'd

built a decentralized, community-based system and dropped it into chaos and expected it to thrive in buildings and neighbourhoods that couldn't support it.

That conversation didn't change our model, but it changed our focus. Mike was right: we couldn't scale chaos. We had to get clear on which buildings and locations actually fit our model. That was when—puns aside—two things came into focus:

First, if the building is too small, under 12 units, the model breaks. For example, a six-unit property doesn't generate enough momentum to motivate a BA or justify a cleaner. But with 12 units or more, the numbers start to work, and so does the model. Also, with security and other community upgrades, the units couldn't absorb those costs without rent being driven up close to market.

Second, external environments matter more than we thought. We'd been through tough buildings before, like 215 Police Call Drive, but Winnipeg proved it doesn't matter how strong your systems are. You can't create community where people don't feel safe walking to their door.

Mike helped us shift from chasing chaos to chasing focus. From proving we could turn around any building to asking a better question: *Should we even be here in the first place?*

You can't fix a broken block with great customer service. You can't build customer confidence where safety is a daily question. Systems only work with a stable foundation.

And that first building in Winnipeg wasn't stable ground.

* * *

The call came in late one afternoon. One of our new customers in Winnipeg had just moved in and was excited. Hopeful.

She'd told the BA this place felt like a reset, a real second chance.

Hope lasted about two days. Then her window got kicked in from the outside. Glass everywhere in her living room. She reported it. We patched it up. A few days later, it happened again. Same unit. Same story. This time, she called me instead of the BA. She didn't sound frustrated. She sounded scared.

"The window's been kicked in again," she said, voice barely above a whisper. "And now the front door's smashed. There are people sleeping in the hallway. I don't know who they are."

I remember standing there, phone to my ear, and my heart just dropped. I wasn't thinking like a founder. I was thinking like a dad. Someone's daughter was living in a war zone. And she was counting on us to fix it.

And if that wasn't enough pressure, did I mention this was all going down during a pandemic? Yeah.

We bought the building from Deloitte, which was representing RBC. The bank had taken it back from the owner during COVID-19, and because of travel restrictions, we toured it over Zoom.

It was clear the place had issues, but we didn't grasp how deep they ran. It had gone into receivership after the previous owner lost control. Only later did we learn why: gangs had taken over. The previous owner had reportedly been told at force, "We run this place." He walked into the bank and handed over the keys.

That was what we bought.

A friend who lived in Winnipeg called me and gave me the bad news. "I don't know how to tell you this, but you bought the worst building in the city." And it felt like it.

But to be clear, we hadn't walked into chaos by accident. We'd chosen it. And to get why, you need to understand what was happening around mid-2022, when something bigger was taking shape in Canada. Housing was entering full-blown crisis mode, especially in urban centres like Halifax, where we were based.

To put it into perspective, Halifax's population surged by over 70,000 people between 2018 and mid-2022, an average growth rate of 4.4% per year. But Halifax wasn't alone. Across Canada, the population surged by more than 2.5 million people between 2021 and 2024, the fastest growth in the country's history. But while demand exploded, housing construction stalled.

That disconnect created a perfect storm: more people, fewer homes, and skyrocketing pressure on the rental market. It was a full-blown crisis.

For many business owners, this would feel like hitting the jackpot. Customers lining up without any effort? Golden opportunity! But I felt uneasy. When demand outpaces supply that quickly, you don't need to market well. You don't need to optimize operations. You don't even need to be particularly good.

And that's the problem. When business is easy, you don't build muscle. You don't build resilience. You don't learn. We all know the famous Warren Buffett quote, "When the tide goes out, you'll discover who's been swimming naked."

I worried we might get complacent. I worried we'd stop innovating. We needed to prepare for the tougher times, when vacancy rates would rise again.

Real estate is cyclical. There are always peaks and valleys. And if we really wanted to pressure-test VIDA, we had to step into a tougher market somewhere outside our backyard.

A friend from my Entrepreneurs' Organization network called and told me about a building for sale in Winnipeg. I hadn't been to Winnipeg in years, but a little research confirmed what I already suspected: it was one of the most challenging urban markets in Canada.

Strict rent controls. Socioeconomic complexity. And vacancy rates in the affordable housing sector were much higher than in other places in the country. It was exactly the kind of place we needed to prove ourselves.

In Winnipeg, you can't raise rents significantly, even on turnover. In some cases, rents are tied to the units themselves, not just the leases. That makes building a sustainable business tough. Combine that with community challenges and higher vacancy rates, and you've got a real test.

It reminded me of when we expanded the security company. Instead of going to Toronto first, I launched in Vancouver—different coast, different time zone, different business culture. I believed that if we could make it work in the hardest market first, everything else would be easier. Most entrepreneurs don't agree with that approach, but when done in bite-sized chunks, it builds resilience and forces innovation.

Winnipeg became the test. And that first building, the one with the kicked-in windows and gang threats, didn't just push us to adapt; it set the tone for how VIDA would tackle complexity head-on. If you can build a team that gets energized by tough challenges, chances are you're going to be successful.

But it also showed us our limits.

We tried everything. We upgraded the locks. Added lighting. Upped security. Leaned into our pillars. But it felt like bailing water out of a sinking ship with a coffee mug.

And sure, VIDA was a pirate ship. We'd handled rough waters before. But this was different. This was like trying to stay afloat while someone was outside, kicking in the windows, and the ocean was pouring in. We were patching holes faster than we could steer.

We'd take one step forward—hire a BA or house a new community partner—and then three steps back. Doors broken. Customers threatened. Progress undone overnight.

We worked with local councils and reached out to police, but the building's exterior environment was beyond what we could reasonably control. In the end, we made the call: sell the building. It was tough but necessary. Because the hard truth is that some communities need deeper systemic change before trust and safety can take root. If we can't live our pillars, we shouldn't own the building.

And that was that.

Except it wasn't.

Because not long after, another opportunity came up in Winnipeg—a seven-building portfolio. Better neighbourhoods. Real potential.

We weren't done with Winnipeg.

* * *

After selling the first building, we knew we could still make the model work there. We just needed the right buildings in the right neighbourhoods.

But that meant something else too: we needed the right capital partner. Someone who could challenge us and help push us further into our next chapter.

I'd already been challenged by the king of real estate. We just weren't ready until now.

Two years earlier, I'd walked into Jon Love's office for the first time. Jon runs KingSett Capital, one of the most respected real estate firms in the country. Some call them the Blackstone of Canada. Back then, I was pitching VIDA like it was already a mature company. I laid out our mission.

Our purpose. Our model. Jon listened closely. Then he looked at me and asked:

"Ron, are you trying to create wealth or change the world?"

I said, "Well, Jon, we can do both."

I thought I understood his question, but I didn't.

What I didn't realize at the time was that Jon wasn't challenging the idea that purpose and profit could coexist. He was trying to understand which one was driving the engine—if we were building a business or more of a mission-driven initiative like a nonprofit.

Either way, his reaction stuck with me. It challenged me in the best way.

Jon didn't kick me out of his office, but the questions he asked that day made it clear I had some growing to do. Some people might've walked away deflated. I spent the flight home reflecting and writing Jon a card. That meeting taught me two things.

First, if VIDA was serious about scaling, we had to show up better prepared when working with sophisticated capital partners.

Second, you can't offer a good answer if you haven't truly understood the question. As former CEO of Procter & Gamble and former Veterans Affairs secretary Bob McDonald, who I had as a guest on the *Scaling Culture* podcast, once put it, "It's not enough to be easy to understand. You need to communicate in a way that's impossible to misunderstand."

In the card, I thanked Jon for the tough questions and included a mug with one of his own quotes printed on the side:

The common trait among all successful people is the same. It's not IQ. It's not just EQ. It's strong adherence to values, respect of others, humility of self, integrity, and building relationships.

I also told him I'd be back in two years.

A few days later, he replied, "Thanks. So thoughtful. We'll see you in two years."

And two years later, here was the seven-building portfolio in Winnipeg—not war zones but solid, stable neighbourhoods where the VIDA model could thrive.

KingSett had just launched an affordability fund, and I knew this was our shot. We pitched them on the investment and partnering with us to acquire it.

And this time, the answer was yes.

VIDA became partners with KingSett. Full circle.

It made sense on every level. They brought deep pockets, high expectations, and serious credibility. Just saying "KingSett is our partner" eliminated 20 questions off the bat. Lenders saw us differently.

And the buildings? Right in the strike zone where the numbers and the model work. All passed our "does it fit" test: minimum 12 units, no full gut jobs, and located in neighbourhoods where people felt safe walking to their front door. Enough scale to justify a cleaner, keep a BA engaged, and run the model the way it was meant to run.

Together, we bought the seven-building, 169-unit portfolio.

It worked. That portfolio became a case study for VIDA. And we were able to lower the vacancy below the industry average in Winnipeg.

The BA model didn't just hold. It shined. And more importantly, we proved we could scale the model without me being there in person. That was a breakthrough.

* * *

In real estate, everyone talks about the need to stay local, to have boots on the ground, someone who knows the neighbourhood. But we'd taken that idea and doubled down. As you can imagine, our model is more than just local. It's hyperlocal local because it's the customers themselves leading the charge.

Operationally, we were getting traction. But marketing was a different game, and in Winnipeg, we were starting from zero. But we had a plan.

Instead of outspending the competition, we would outthink them. I did what I always do when learning anything new: I dove into the research. I started listening to podcasts and learning about SEO, pay-per-click, and other social strategies. I heard on a podcast that the number one thing you need to do is get to a customer before your competition. You have to have call centres ready, and everything needs to move fast.

And I remember thinking, *There's no way we'll win that game. Not against massive companies with million-dollar ad budgets.* So we went the other way. We went scrappy, smart, and specific. We built what we now call our Golden Triangle marketing approach.

The first side of the triangle? Winning the media through newsjacking.

Back in 2017, I came across David Meerman Scott, and his strategy stuck. The idea was simple: when there's a news story tied to a problem your business solves, you jump in and hijack it. You reach out to the media, comment on the story, and explain how your business can solve the issue. You add value. Offer a solution. Reframe the narrative.

One case study stood out: Lindsay Lohan was going bankrupt, and a luxury handbag resale company offered to fix and auction off her designer bags. *The Washington Post* picked it up. Then *The New York Times.* That luxury handbag company didn't pay for advertising. *They became the story.*

We used that same approach when we launched in Winnipeg. If a story broke about housing challenges, we reached out to reporters and told them, "Here's how VIDA is solving that exact issue." It worked. Media attention became our runway.

The second part of our strategy is customers as fans.

We built systems to spotlight our residents, turning everyday wins into public celebrations. Someone becomes a Community Contractor? We shout them out. If a BA organizes a cleanup? We film it. A resident buys their first car or lands a new job? We cheer, and sometimes we throw in a rent credit.

And then we asked ourselves, *Why stop there?*

In real estate, if a customer wants to leave their unit early, most landlords hold them to the lease. It doesn't matter if they're moving to help an elderly family member or buy their first home. "Too bad, so sad" is the standard line. But we flipped that on its head.

We thought, *What if we celebrated milestones instead of sticking people with penalties?* Buying your first home is hard enough in Canada, so if we hear a customer is taking that step, we break the lease for them. Not only that, but we give them $350 to help with moving costs, and we celebrate with them.

Same if they get a raise or a new job or head back to work after retirement. We've given out rent credits for all of it. It's what community does. We recognize each other's progress.

We even have our own in-house journalist, Joel Goodman, who helps those customer stories come to life. He brings heart. Dives deep. Then he puts pen to paper before handing them off to the marketing team, who make sure the impact is seen far and wide. We're not just building housing. We're building momentum. Helping customers gain skills, earn income, and get celebrated for the very milestones the industry usually punishes.

And in doing so, we're turning customers into real fans.

Fans of VIDA. Fans of their community. Fans of their own potential. When you have fans like we do, they post, share, and reshare stories, which does the marketing for you.

Today, we've taken this to a whole new level. As we grew, we wanted to create the space for bigger celebrations. So we launched the VIDA Impact Awards, a night to honour the people building community every day. We rented out a movie theatre. Sent formal invites. Set up a swag station. Even served popcorn!

The room was packed with Building Ambassadors, Community Contractors, partners, and suppliers. Then we handed the mic to our people. One by one, they took the stage, recognized for organizing cleanups, mentoring neighbours, fixing units, and showing up.

It was dignity. It was recognition. It was joy on a big screen.

Now for the third and final side of the triangle: community partners.

We reach out to suppliers—painters, plumbers, local restaurants, and small businesses—because we believe the community doesn't stop at the building. We offer discounts, frontline access to submit an application, and a chance to be part of something bigger. We save on marketing, and the community partner gains loyal customers. Together, we strengthen the local economy. It's a total win-win.

With media wins, customer stories, and community partners all working in sync, our Golden Triangle gave us traction in a brand-new city. It didn't cost much, but it hit deep. Our strategy showcased what is possible when you put customers at the centre of the model.

But our marketing efforts were planting the seeds of something bigger. They were the start of a global brand rewriting the rules of affordable housing.

I went to great lengths to learn how brands became platforms, how they built something that transcended their product, something people actually wanted to be part of. I even spent time on Necker Island with Sir Richard Branson to learn how he built the Virgin brand. I wanted to understand how you scale without losing soul, how you stay human, even as you go global.

One thing I knew for sure was that strategy gave us traction. Discipline would take us further.

* * *

As we continued our partnership with KingSett, one thing was obvious: VIDA was still a pirate ship—scrappy, fast, and unorthodox. KingSett was a navy vessel—organized, disciplined, sharp. Could we sail together as direct owners of assets?

In the early stages of the partnership, we had friction. Their reporting standards were intense. At first it felt like busywork—metrics we didn't use for decision-making. Our team was overwhelmed. But in hindsight, some of that reporting was exactly what we needed. It brought structure. It forced discipline. And it helped us grow up as an organization.

Today, every KPI we track has a purpose. And a lot of that came from Jon and the discipline KingSett brought to the table.

Jon doesn't just invest capital. He gives his time and wisdom. During our partnership, I had the privilege to join one of his fundraisers for multiple sclerosis, rappelling down a Toronto skyscraper in support. Someone asked, "Why are you doing this? It's not your cause."

My answer was simple: "Because Jon's my partner. And

when your partner calls, you show up. You go all in, no questions asked."

That's the kind of partner I want to be. One who shows up when it's important, even if it's outside the scope of the deal. That's what it means to have real connection.

Eventually, we bought KingSett out of the portfolio. A major milestone. That partnership with KingSett marked a turning point, but it also was a test of VIDA's maturity. Because of them, we emerged sharper. Stronger. And ready for what came next.

Which was what we needed. Because what came next wasn't a seven-building portfolio. It was over 1,000 units. A $100 million test of everything we'd learned. A portfolio no one else had figured out how to operate at scale.

And this time we were ready.

CHAPTER NINE

Who the Hell Is VIDA?

EVERY FOUNDER REMEMBERS WHEN THEY HAD THEIR first transformational deal. Not just for the business but for how others see them. The moment when the stakes shift from proving they can do it to proving they can do it at scale.

For VIDA, that moment was Telus.

Up to that point, VIDA was still the underdog. The disruptor. The team with a bold mission and a growing track record but not yet a seat at the table with the industry's biggest players. The Telus portfolio changed that.

It wasn't just a big deal. It was the deal. Over 1,000 units. Nearly $100 million. And we were going up against giants. We didn't just win the deal. We redefined how these deals could get done: fast, bold, and anchored in values.

Winning the deal showed that our model could not only compete; it could deliver. It could scale. And it could offer a real solution to one of the biggest challenges in this country: preserving deeply affordable housing for working-class Canadians. Because once it's gone, it's gone forever.

What follows isn't just a story about how we outmanoeuvred major players to win the deal.

It's about how we executed one of the largest affordable housing transactions in the country and used it to sharpen our strike zone and lay the groundwork for what's possible at scale.

* * *

Word was spreading: a massive portfolio was about to hit the market. Telus Pensions Master Trust was getting out, off-loading a bundle of vintage affordable housing buildings from the 1970s and '80s. They'd brought in CBRE to lead the sale, a sign they were serious. Too many challenges. They were ready to off-load the whole thing.

And they weren't the only ones. Across Canada, pension funds and REITs were pulling out of this asset class. Rising operating costs, from interest rates to inflation, were cutting into profits. Deferred maintenance was driving up capital expenditures.

The whole thing was too fragmented. One group owned the building, while another managed the assets and another operated the building, with everyone trying to squeeze out their own return but no one actually accountable to the customer.

Supply was tight, but demand was tighter. And with fewer unit turns, operators couldn't chase market rents. The typical value-add strategy didn't work if tenants weren't moving. No turnover meant no upside. And without upside, investors weren't biting.

The pressure was building, and attention was starting to follow. Media coverage had zeroed in on bad operators and spiking rents. Nobody wanted to be seen as the villain. These weren't just real estate assets anymore. They were reputational liabilities.

I knew we were the right operator for these buildings. No one else had figured them out. Three owners had already tried and failed.

Six months earlier, Natalie and I were at our summer home in Chester, Nova Scotia, for New Year's. Our new neighbours invited us to a party. That was where I met Hugh Goodday.

He was really sharp. A high performer who had worked as a lawyer with Blake, Cassels & Graydon, one of the top firms in Toronto. More recently, he'd worked in the UK, managing large Canadian clients. During the pandemic, like a lot of people, he'd moved back to Nova Scotia.

We started chatting, and he told me he was looking to pivot to something more strategic, long term. He wanted a different pace, more time for his future family and sailing. "It's time for a change," he said. "I'm looking for something that gives me stability but also room to grow."

I liked him immediately.

I told him about the Telus deal. "We're going after it," I said. "It's big. Transformational. And I think we can pull it off."

Hugh raised an eyebrow. "That sounds like a big deal for a company your size."

"It is," I said. "And I think you could help us get there. You should come work with us."

He didn't say yes right away. He weighed his options. He could've easily walked into a top-tier law firm and made double what we could offer. But what he saw in VIDA was a sense of purpose. Building something from the ground up. The chance to have ownership and potential equity—to learn the business, the strategy—meant more than a big salary ever could.

The next day, I walked into the office and told Eric, "I met a really smart guy last night, and I think we should hire him."

Eric gave me a look. "What does he do?"

"He's a lawyer," I said.

Eric clicked his pen. That's his deep-thinking tell and usually a sign he doesn't agree. "Ron, at this point in the business, don't you think it might make more sense to hire someone to answer the phones? Maybe a secretary would be more helpful right now."

I laughed. "I hear you. But if we're going to grow the way we plan to, we need top-tier people. We're going to be acquiring a lot, possibly selling noncore buildings, forming new partnerships, and potentially structuring funds. Hugh's securities law background is invaluable. We can hire a secretary later. Right now we need someone who can help us build this business."

A few days later, he came in to meet Eric. After the meeting, I turned to Eric and asked, "Well?"

Eric grinned. "Let's hire him!"

It turned out to be one of the best decisions we've made. Hugh didn't just bring legal expertise. He raised the bar for everyone. He's meticulous and thoughtful, and he holds all of us accountable, including me. I often say, "He's the yin to my yang." I don't love details, but Hugh thrives on them. He breaks things down and makes them simple so I can cut through the noise and focus on what really matters.

In 2023, VIDA achieved a milestone I'm incredibly proud of: we became a certified B Corp. And Hugh led the charge.

For those unfamiliar, B Corp certification is issued by B Lab and is a globally recognized seal that proves a company is committed to doing good while doing business. It's a full-spectrum evaluation: governance, employee treatment, environmental impact, and community involvement. You don't just check a box. You prove you're living your values.

We scored an impressive 96%. Sure, we got dinged for not having a formal electronics recycling policy, but that was an easy fix. Becoming a B Corp validated everything we've been building. It set VIDA apart in an industry where transparency and ethics are often afterthoughts.

Hugh is now an equity partner and serves as VIDA's president. His impact has been tremendous.

And we had barely hired him when the Telus deal went into overdrive.

At the time, VIDA had units across Nova Scotia, New Brunswick, and Manitoba. We were growing, but the Telus deal was a proving ground, our chance to redefine what scale means in the affordable housing sector.

We were working with our two main lenders, BMO and Timbercreek. Timbercreek introduced me to Price Capital Partners (PCP), which included Mike Foy. Mike had already helped sharpen how we thought about scaling. I trusted him completely. There was no way I was going into this without him in the mix.

Starlight, Canada's largest landlord, with 60,000 units, was one of the other bidders. A few others were circling too. All sophisticated players. I knew we had to stand out. I also knew we had to move fast.

I knew the terms that would get us there: a 60-day, no-conditions close and a $3 million nonrefundable deposit. I'd put up $1 million of my own money and guarantee the remaining $2 million for partners I hadn't even met in person yet (thanks to the pandemic).

Of course, everyone had an opinion: Hugh, our external counsel, our advisors. "Why are you taking on their risk? Why would you guarantee their funds?" they all asked. Naturally, I called John Risley.

"John, I need your take here. Am I crazy?"

John didn't hesitate. "They're entrepreneurs. They've built businesses. They're not walking away from a huge deal to try to make two million bucks. I don't know these guys, but based on their history and current holdings, they will want to build a large business here."

He was right. And I'd done my homework. I knew the capital structures of the other bidders. I also knew they couldn't move as fast as we could. This wasn't reckless. It was calculated.

The pandemic had reshaped how deals got done. Site visits weren't happening. The sellers had already commissioned inspections, environmental reports, and full vendor documentation. We trusted the data, and we trusted the relationships.

It was go time:

I called BMO. "Can you close in sixty days?"

"Yes."

Timbercreek. "Can you support this and close on time?"

"Yes."

Lawyers. "Can you work fast?"

"Tight, but doable."

The only real wild card was the appraisal. I paused before making the call. Normally I build the relationship before making the ask, but we didn't have time.

I called the appraiser directly. "We don't know each other," I said, "but here's the number we need to hit. I'm confident the value's there. Can you help us get it done?"

He chuckled. "Nice to meet you too. I think you'll be fine."

We submitted our bid: $87.5 million. No conditions, with $3 million nonrefundable.

And let's be clear: what we submitted wasn't a bid. It was a vision.

We told the story of VIDA: our values, our model, our commitment to long-term affordability. We used our mission to our advantage. We didn't position VIDA as just another buyer. We made it clear we were the *right* buyer.

These units were incredibly affordable. Most bidders would've renovated and raised rents. We leaned into that reality.

"If you sell to them," we said, "your tenants might be priced out, and it could hit the headlines."

We also included something unheard of in this industry: a post-close meeting. Sixty days after closing, the sellers had to meet with us for a debrief. I told our lawyer, "We're doing it. Put it in."

He didn't even try to hide the disbelief. "Ron, that's highly unlikely. I've never seen it happen, and it's not how this industry works."

That kind of relational clause was unheard of. Most real estate deals are hyper-transactional. People disappear after the ink dries. But that's not VIDA's style.

Then I got the call. CBRE came back with a game-changing update. "We're recommending your bid."

I felt everything: pride, panic, adrenalin, excitement. A part of me probably hoped we wouldn't win. But the bigger part—the part that loves risk, impact, and transformation—was fired up. This was the moment.

To get this deal done, we knew everything had to be airtight: strategy, structure, execution. So we implemented a key communication cadence: we pulled everyone together for weekly calls. Lawyers, lenders, partners. Everyone.

In this industry, the norm is long email chains and siloes.

We couldn't risk the old industry ways for this deal. We needed to flush out issues in real time, with everyone at the table.

Radical transparency. No finger-pointing. If something was stuck, we fixed it together. Everyone owned the outcome.

But then it happened. Just as things were moving forward, 30 days before closing, I got a call from Geoff McTait at Timbercreek.

"Ron, we've got a problem."

My stomach dropped. "What is it?"

"The board rejected the structure. We can't move forward."

Timbercreek was supposed to bring in equity from PCP and manage the debt. But since PCP was also a shareholder in Timbercreek at the time, the board flagged a conflict of interest. Just like that. No equity, no loan.

So there we were, 30 days out, and the money was gone. I was stunned. We'd lined everything up, and the whole thing was unravelling. I hung up the phone and sat there, trying to breathe.

We had to find another way. Fast.

That was when Geoff stepped up.

Geoff, who could visibly pass as the Ben Stiller of commercial lending, is one of those guys who never looks rattled. Humble, incredibly sophisticated, the kind of steady hand you want when things go sideways.

He didn't flinch. "Give me a week. I'll get this sorted," he said.

I didn't sleep that entire week. It was brutal. A total nailbiter. The deal was suddenly beyond my control. And for someone who's used to solving problems by diving straight into the fire, that kind of limbo eats at you.

By Friday afternoon, after a full week of waiting, I was emotionally tapped.

That day, my good friend Shaun Majumder was in town. We hadn't seen each other for a while, so he came by my house in Halifax. We were out on the patio, the sun warm on our backs, about to crack a beer and catch up like old times.

But I wasn't fully present.

The weight of the Telus deal was in the background of every laugh, every pause. My mind kept drifting, still pacing through what-ifs.

Then my phone rang.

It was Geoff.

I looked at Shaun, held up a finger, and stepped away to answer. I barely got a hello in before Geoff's voice came through, calm, steady, certain.

"Ron, we're good to go."

His words washed over me like a wave.

He'd found a new path forward and had gotten everyone back to the table—just in time.

This was a huge win. Getting this done would be proof that VIDA could go toe to toe with the biggest players in Canadian real estate. And it was a big win for affordable housing.

I closed my eyes and let it sink in. Then I walked back to the patio, looked at Shaun, and finally cracked that beer. Fully present.

* * *

Winning the Telus deal was a milestone. But it also came with a mirror.

This was our chance to show the country exactly who we were. To prove that VIDA's model could grow without compromise. That deeply affordable housing could be preserved not just at scale but with precision, intention, and pride.

And now, with over 1,000 new units on the books, it was time to deliver.

Real estate is full of operators who say the right things until the ink is dry. They buy everything, hold on to anything, and let ego or momentum override strategy if they even have one. That's the danger with big moves. You lose your edge. You drift from the strategy that made you different in the first place.

We weren't going to become just another group that talks big and delivers average.

This meant we had to be honest once again about which buildings fit our focus and which didn't. So we rolled up our sleeves and got strategic. Fast.

We went through the portfolio piece by piece, identifying anything that didn't align. That meant selling off buildings under 12 units, properties that needed excessive capital expenditures, rural locations with no clear path for reinvestment, and buildings with particularly challenging customer bases.

Our method combined two very different approaches. Eric brought the analytical horsepower, diving deep in Excel, modelling scenarios, and stress-testing every variable. I'd glance at one of his spreadsheets and get dizzy. But he loved it.

Meanwhile, I had my own system. Unconventional, of course. Call it street smarts with a *slice* of sophistication.

And I mean that literally. I'd head straight to the local pizza shop near the buildings we were looking at. As everyone knows, real estate is a local business. If you want the real story, talk to the delivery drivers dropping slices at 10 at night.

Think about it. They know where the stairwells reek of Pine-Sol versus weed. Where the lights are always broken and the intercom never works. But they also know the deeper stuff: where doors get slammed in your face, where the vibe is off, where safety's hanging by a flickering hallway light. The places they won't send new drivers to. Where they'd never let their own kids live.

Every time I showed up at a shop, I used the same talk track.

"Is the delivery guy around?"

I usually got a confused look. "Uh, is everything okay?"

"Totally fine," I said." "Just a couple of questions."

When the driver showed up, I introduced myself. "Hi. I'm Ron Lovett. I'm looking at buildings in the area, but I need your help." Then I'd ask, "Do you have kids?"

If yes, I'd hit him with two more. "Here's a list of buildings. Which ones would you not let your kids live in? And which ones would make you feel uncomfortable delivering to?"

The intel I got from those conversations was gold. You can run the numbers all day—capex budgets, rent rolls—but that doesn't tell you if the space behind the walls is safe. This was more than due diligence. It was deep-dish intelligence, stuff no conventional process could ever uncover. It reminded me of when I used to do my own reconnaissance in my security days.

It works every time.

We identified all the noncore buildings in the Telus portfolio, and we had to move fast to off-load them. The market was still hot. Interest rates were hovering around 2.5%.

That was when Mike Foy's network came into play.

Through him, we were introduced to a group called Whitehall. This was their first time doing business on the East Coast. At the time, they had around 700 to 800 units in their portfolio and were looking to grow. We were offering them 300 units from our noncore list—almost half their size. That kind of jump could go sideways fast without the right support.

In real estate, sales are usually clean-cut. You pass the asset and move on. Relationships end at closing.

But we saw it differently. Even selling noncore buildings was a chance to lead the industry in a better direction. We didn't just unload assets. We curated the handoff. Because if the next owner failed, so would our reputation. And that is incredibly important to us.

One of the best lessons I learned from John Risley, when he sold Clearwater, was this: if you want a deal to succeed, wrap it in a bow. That means eliminating friction, building alignment early, and making sure everyone knows exactly what they're walking into.

Where most operators play it close to the chest, John's approach was the opposite. Set the table early. Bring everyone in. Walk them through it—literally. He told me how, before a single term sheet was signed, he hosted all parties at his home for dinner. No pitch decks. No lawyers. Just an open conversation about how the deal could actually work for everyone.

It was unheard of but brilliant. Most people grind to get a deal done by working against each other. John treated them like partners and helped them get the deal done.

I loved his strategy. And we took the same red-carpet approach when we worked with Whitehall.

We helped them every step of the way in closing the deal.

We introduced them to our bankers, John Keating and Geoff Pearson from BMO, who had just helped us close $75 million of debt for the Telus deal. We shared our insurance contacts, our property management referrals, and all our suppliers. We even structured a vendor take-back for $4.5 million.

Months later, after COVID-19 restrictions were finally lifted, we closed the deal with Whitehall. We had a proper closing dinner for Telus at my place—bankers, lenders, and partners, all packed around the table. Geoff from Timbercreek flew in, and midway through the night, he put down his glass, looked around, and said, "I had lunch with a friend from Slate after the Telus deal closed. Let's just say I think they are still licking their wounds."

"What do you mean?" I asked.

Slate Asset Management, a large institution, was one of our competitors in the bid. Slate had been banking on this portfolio to launch into the Canadian multifamily market. They thought they had it locked. When they lost, they were stunned.

Geoff leaned in. "Apparently, they all piled into a boardroom, trying to figure out what the hell happened. One of them goes, 'Someone find out right now: who the hell is VIDA?'"

Laughter filled the room.

"So they googled you, Ron. They found the story about you working with Justin Bieber."

The room was buzzing now.

He continued, "And then someone said, 'You mean to tell me we just lost a hundred-million-dollar deal to Justin Bieber's bodyguard?'"

The whole table burst out laughing.

Underneath the punchline was a deeper truth: we didn't deliver a bid. We delivered a blueprint for how a mission-driven buyer could rewrite the playbook and still win.

* * *

Telus pushed us to hone that focus. Over time, we realized that bigger wasn't always better. Some of the large buildings with 50-plus units that we first saw as wins started to strain the core of our BA model: personal connection, clear ownership, local pride, and accountability. With too many doors, that personal connection starts to break down.

So we've tested what happens when multiple BAs support a single building, watching closely to see where the model holds and where it starts to bend. In some cases, it creates confusion for both customers and team members. Whom do you go to for what? Who owns the garbage area? When everyone's trying to help, no one really owns it. And in this model, ownership matters. That sense of pride and clarity is what brings the whole thing to life.

And we hear it all the time: "Why aren't you buying my building? Why aren't you doing more of X or Y?"

And the truth is that we'd love to do it all. We'd love to preserve every deeply affordable six- or eight-unit walk-up. But if it doesn't fit our strike zone, if we can't properly serve customers living in it over the long term, we can't be there. We'd have to raise rents just to keep the lights on. And that's not who we are.

If we want to revolutionize affordable communities at scale, we can't be everything to everyone.

For me, one of the most powerful parts of the Telus deal, looking back, is that we did exactly what we said we would. And in doing that, we proved something rare in this industry: deeply affordable housing can be preserved, and it can work.

But not long after Telus, the economic pressure turned up.

Inflation spiked. Operating costs shot through the roof. Rent caps held firm.

We needed more than discipline. We needed a new engine.

PART 4

Gloves Off, All In

CHAPTER 10

An Engine to Go Further

TO ANYONE TIRED OF WAITING FOR THE SYSTEM TO FIX itself: read on!

We know middle-class Canadians are feeling it. Groceries are up. Gas too. Rents are rising faster than incomes. Housing, once meant to provide safety, stability, and pride, has become the anchor pulling people under.

We felt the crisis long before the headlines started reporting it. Inflation didn't start the problem, but it widened the gaps, pulling in more working-class households and families. And it created the need for a new kind of model. VIDA's model.

We created VIDA to revolutionize affordable housing because we'd already seen what happened when systems fail the people they're supposed to serve. VIDA is proof that housing can be decentralized, led from the front lines, and still be disciplined, scalable, and centred on the customer. That trust can be rebuilt. That communities can be safe, proud, and affordable—not by accident but by design.

A system for the people. Built by the people.

The economic pressure hasn't let up. But neither have

we. We've held the line by tightening our model and staying laser focused on what works. And we've proven that purpose and performance can go hand in hand. But when costs keep rising—insurance, interest, taxes, utilities—even the strongest model gets stretched.

We needed more than grit. We needed a new engine that could take everything we'd proven and push it further with precision, with partners, and without losing what made it work in the first place.

So that's what we created: a vehicle built to match the size of the problem and the scale of our ambition. A system that creates value and opportunity for the people who live in it and the partners who help make it possible.

If you believe every person deserves a safe, affordable place to call home, then this chapter is for you.

* * *

When we acquired the properties from Telus, the world was changing. Fast.

Inflation surged. Interest rates jumped from 2.5% to nearly 8%. Utility and property tax costs spiked. Every dial on the board was going up.

The financing environment flipped. Cap rates held steady even as borrowing costs soared, putting pressure not just on new deals but on the capital our existing partners had already deployed. Buy, stabilize, refinance in two years wasn't going to work anymore.

In real estate, what most tenants don't realize—but VIDA customers do—is that when operating costs go up, rents need to adjust. That's how the owners of those buildings stay afloat.

But in some provinces, new rent caps were introduced,

freezing our ability to adjust to cover operating costs. Suddenly, we were losing $85 per unit per month. Rent increases were capped at 2%, which meant we could only raise an $800 rent by $16. But costs had climbed 20–50%. It felt like trying to stop a flood with a paper towel.

For most, this would have been the end of the story—a reason to scale back, retreat, fold. But VIDA was built for turning friction into fuel. For moments when the old systems break and someone has to show a better way forward.

So when the economic pressure turned up, we didn't flinch. We adapted.

I started where I always did: making sure the foundation was sound. I called our banks to restructure our debt. I called partners and suppliers to renegotiate terms. We leaned into every relationship we had, from landscaping to paint, to lock in stability where we could.

Here's what that looks like in action: we don't just hire vendors. We build ecosystems.

Take lawn care or snow removal. We intentionally seek out small, up-and-coming local players in the space. Reputable companies with something to prove. Companies that bring hustle and heart without the bloated overhead of big national players.

We offer long-term contracts—three to five years—so they can plan, invest, and grow. We lock in pricing to fight inflation. We share our systems and connect them with housing, staffing, and even business support if they need it. We treat them like partners, not suppliers, because revolutionizing affordable communities doesn't stop at the buildings. It lifts the entire ecosystem.

With the basics locked in, we turned to two priorities: focusing on a long-term growth strategy built on patient capital and staying ahead of inflation by doubling down on what we could control.

We started by looking inward, at repairs, utilities, labour. Most of our biggest challenges could be influenced from the ground up. So we went straight to the front lines, to the people closest to the problems: our Building Ambassadors.

Up until early 2024, the BA role was pretty siloed. BAs had the autonomy to make decisions, manage spending, and handle repairs, but there wasn't much structure. No clear budgets, no shared goals, and not much collaboration across buildings. But rising costs didn't just create pressure. They revealed opportunity.

This was a clear systems problem. Repair and maintenance spending had spiked. Finance froze all nonessential spending for 60 days. Customers were frustrated. BAs were confused. The whole thing needed a reset.

We needed to balance spending without losing the speed, customer trust, and ownership that made the model work. So we zoomed out.

We brought the challenge to our HR Advisory Council. These were leaders from Southwest Airlines, Amazon, Zappos, and NASCAR. Not real estate folks. Culture experts. People who knew how to scale teams, lead, and design organizational structures without losing their soul.

Their advice was to stop looking in the rearview. Lagging financial data wouldn't cut it. If we wanted to preserve VIDA's model in the face of rising costs, we needed leading indicators—real-time signals from the front lines about how people, systems, and spending were holding up.

So we turned one of our Halifax communities into a 60-day pilot. A real-world test of what a decentralized team model could do.

We brought together a handful of trusted BAs in Halifax, each running their own building, just a few blocks apart. They'd never worked as a team before. Now they would while testing one simple idea: what if local leaders could pool their budgets, priorities, and problem-solving? No new layers of oversight. Just clarity, a team structure, and transparency.

We gave them a clear repairs and maintenance target per unit. A platform to share tips and resources. A designated "Team Captain" to lead. And we gamified the whole thing.

They didn't just crush it. They changed the game.

Spending dropped from $110 per unit to $23. Customer satisfaction stayed high. Paint was pooled. Smart fixes were shared. One BA even came up with a $12 spray solution to seal cracks in tubs, saving $1,500 per unit by avoiding full replacements. The idea caught on instantly and was shared across the team's group chat.

They competed and had fun, all while VIDA saved thousands that we could pass on to our customers in savings, *even after* paying out bonuses for staying under budget. But something even more interesting happened.

One month later, when they earned a surplus, we gave them a choice: divvy up the bonus based on individual performance or split it evenly. They went with the even split. No flexing. No fuss. Just one crew, one goal.

The surplus wasn't just leftover budget. It was proof that a decentralized, team-based model could drive real financial results without compromising service. And a reminder that great systems don't control people. They *unlock* them.

We turned the pilot into a playbook. We grouped BAs into local teams, each covering a cluster of 150 to 250 units. Every BA still owned their building, but now they were part of a squad with a shared budget, team support, and regular communication. That shift made everyday decisions smarter. Teams pooled materials, shared fixes, and kept each other sharp.

We officially changed the name Community Leaders to Team Captains. These leaders drive team performance, provide mentorship, support onboarding, and keep everyone aligned.

Each team includes 8–10 BAs, supported by a Team Captain. Team Captains get monthly dashboards with financials and performance scorecards so they know where the team stands and where to step up. It's clean and clear, and it frees up BAs to focus on what matters most: customer service and community leadership.

The final touch? Each team chose its own name rooted in the neighbourhood. The pilot group became The OGs. That identity mattered and gave them rocket fuel.

I'm convinced a group of seasoned real estate pros wouldn't have come up with this, but our HR Council did. It didn't come from a playbook. It was built, tested, and brought to life on the front lines, where real change always starts.

With the team model locked in, we turned to the next set of experts in the fight against rising costs: our customers.

* * *

When inflation hits, most companies raise prices and cut back. VIDA's average rent for a two-bedroom, including heat and hot water, was around $965. And we weren't about to pile on more. Our customers were already stretched. So we doubled down on savings through community-led cost control and partnerships that delivered real value.

Some of that groundwork was already in motion. Through

onboarding, we were building a co-stakeholder mindset, educating customers on things like waste sorting and cutting down on utility use. Why? Because utilities are one of the biggest drivers of operating costs. And when operating costs go up, rent pressure follows. If we want to keep rents low, we need customers to be part of the solution.

But the success of the team model gave us a new lens. If gamification worked there, why not here? So we gave customers a reason to care and a reason to play along.

We launched our first contest: Save Water to Win. The concept was that water is expensive, and things like long showers drive up the bill. The goal: get everyone to cut back, together.

Leading the charge was my seven-year-old daughter, Georgia. Because, really, what better way is there to spark a behaviour shift than getting schooled by the youth of our generation? We made a video showing her scolding me for taking long showers and leaving the tap running while brushing my teeth. She didn't just get the message. She delivered it.

One person joked, "Wait. If I cut my shower from 45 minutes to 10, we all win?" Exactly. And Georgia would've told you the same thing.

That spirit caught on.

We ran Earth Day initiatives like Every Action Counts, where customers shared stories about cleaning up their community or showing kindness to a neighbour. One lucky winner got six months of free rent. Yes: six months. We even recorded the call where we told them in real time and shared it with the community. The result was real buy-in and cleaner, kinder, more connected communities. And we cut costs on third-party spring cleanups while we were at it.

Even one of our toughest properties was transformed through a Cash for Trash initiative. Customers guessed where waste belonged, won small prizes, and learned proper sorting. We supported them with multilingual guides, community cleanups, music, and activities for kids. It worked because it was fun, visible, and rooted in community.

Behind the scenes, we used teams to scale these initiatives strategically. Each team got scorecards that track leading indicators, like waste costs, utility spikes, and more. If we saw a surge in water use or waste costs increasing at one building, we launched a contest and got the community involved.

But we didn't stop there. We looked for ways to reduce costs by adding value in ways no real estate owners in Canada had previously touched.

By 2024, more than 6.5 million Canadians didn't have a family doctor. Healthcare access was out of reach for many of our customers, especially newcomers and gig workers. So we partnered with Telus Health to offer virtual care. What started as an employee benefit became a community lifeline. One customer told us, "I've been trying to get a family doctor for three years. This was a lifesaver."

We also cold-called Amazon Business. No connections. Just a hunch. That was when I was linked up with Evan Jones and then Matt Wright. We pitched them on helping VIDA scale smart product sourcing like bulk cleaning supplies and Bluetooth locks at scale. They leaned in. Together we built customer upgrade plans where customers could buy things like digital locks with small monthly payments, better security, and shared upside.

Amazon even made a video about the partnership, putting their brand behind ours. Today customers can buy essentials like soap and paper towels at discounted rates through VIDA's Amazon portal.

VIDA responds to rising costs while driving margin not by

charging more but by providing more value through innovation. And our partnerships are still growing, not just to survive this moment but to prove a different future is possible.

With these and other types of innovative solutions in play, it was now time to focus on growth again. We needed fuel. Long-term. Patient. Purpose-aligned. The kind strong enough to take everything we'd built—systems, proven results—and carry it across the country.

We knew we couldn't just take on more debt. Interest rates, inflation, and rent caps made it impossible to return money to partners quickly.

So we started thinking differently about long-term capital or even launching our own fund. But one thing was clear: when you're building a model this different, the partner matters just as much as the product.

For this next chapter of growth, we weren't just looking for capital. We were looking for alignment. A shared belief in what housing could be and how business could do better. And for us, one name kept coming up: BMO.

They were already our lender and an incredible banking partner. But this was bigger than banking. Their mission said it all: Boldly Grow the Good in business and life. Not just words on a wall but a real commitment to strengthening communities, expanding access to housing, and backing bold, purpose-driven ideas.

They already felt like the right fit. I just needed to get in the room.

It was time for one of the boldest moves of my career: *a beer, a bet, and a shot at something much bigger*.

* * *

I was in Florida over Christmas, hanging out with my wife's cousin Mark, who works with BMO in New York. We were drinking beers and talking shop, and I was raving about BMO.

"Man, BMO's been fantastic for us. Such a great partner," I said casually. Then I added, "You know, I'd love to meet Darryl White, the CEO."

Mark nearly spit out his beer. "Ha! Yeah, right. Good luck with that."

I locked eyes with him. "What makes you say that?"

He laughed harder. "Ron, they just bought Bank of the West, one of the biggest banks in North America. No way you're meeting Darryl White."

"Wanna bet?"

He raised his beer: "A hundred bucks. US. No Canadian Monopoly money."

Challenge accepted. For my first move, I sent Darryl a copy of my first book, *Outrageous Empowerment*, wrapped in custom VIDA paper, with a handwritten note. I fired off emails. I worked every angle.

As expected, I got the usual "Darryl's travelling," "He's unavailable." But I wasn't going anywhere.

This wasn't about the bet anymore. To even ask for investment at this scale, for a model that could reshape housing in Canada, we needed real relationships at the top.

I learned that lesson the hard way.

A few years earlier, I was on BMO's Client Advisory Council. I knew the head of commercial lending, the COO, and my local rep. I felt like I was locked in. But one by one, they moved on. New roles. New banks. And just like that, I was back to zero.

I told myself *never again*. If you're building something big, you can't just know the org chart. You have to build relationships that outlast it.

So I kept pushing.

And then, one day, my assistant called me. "You did it."

"Did what?"

"You're in. Darryl's team reached out. You've got a lunch meeting with Darryl White—plus two vice chairs, the VP and head of commercial banking for North America, the senior VP of real estate finance, and the managing director of real estate investment banking."

I paused. "Wait. All of them?"

He laughed. "Yeah. Looks like you stirred the pot. You're getting the full table."

This wasn't lunch. It was a summit.

So we swung big. The truth was, if we were serious about future growth, we needed a vehicle to get there. A fund was the answer: $300 million to preserve 7,000 units across Canada.

The timing was brutal. Capital was frozen. No one was writing cheques. But demand for affordable housing was off the charts.

We had the platform. What we needed was an anchor. Someone willing to go first and take a bet, not just on us but on a better model for housing. Because let's be real: no one gets fired for betting on Blackstone. But backing a startup in Halifax at the worst possible time in the market?

You've got to be bold.

BMO was bold.

They have a real commitment to strengthening the communities they serve, creating opportunity, removing barriers to housing, and backing bold, purpose-driven ideas.

We worked tirelessly to prepare for that meeting—everything from learning how to structure a fund to refining the pitch. We needed a name. A hook. A story.

Canadian NOAH (Naturally Occurring Affordable Housing) Preservation Fund.

Clean. Meaningful. Timely.

Core-plus returns wrapped in impact. This wasn't just a theory or fresh idea. VIDA was already doing it. In 2023 alone, VIDA returned $1.6 million directly into the neighbourhoods we serve. And not just in dollars but in *real opportunities*. We trained customers to paint, patch drywall, turn units, and build real skills. This wasn't fluff. It was the *S* in ESG (Environmental, Social, and Governance) in action.

When I walked into that meeting on the sixty-eighth floor in Toronto, I was more prepared than I'd ever been in my life.

Brian Tobin, one of the vice chairs and former premier of Newfoundland, walked in. I'd met him years earlier under tragic circumstances when his son was violently attacked while working for my security company. It was a heavy memory, but we'd built a bond through it. Seeing him there felt like a full-circle moment.

The room was packed with power players. Darryl couldn't make it at the last minute, which meant I was out $100. But that didn't matter. We had the right audience. And Brian lit up the room. I could tell he was proud. An East Coaster sitting at the table with the big leagues, pushing something bold. Something real.

We pitched the fund. Not just the structure but the purpose and impact behind it. A long-hold, purpose-built model that was stabilized on day one. Buy on Friday, collect rent on Monday. Light repairs. No evictions. No flipping. Just long-term, sustainable, affordable housing.

The negotiations that followed were the most intense I've ever experienced. It was like corporate chess—learning how the machine moves, how capital flows, who needs to say yes before anything happens. Frustrating and fascinating all at once.

As I write this, the journey with BMO continues—but this next chapter is all about patient capital and finding partners who value both impact and return.

That's why we know BMO is the right anchor investor for our fund. They've already been with us through thick and thin. They saw firsthand that it's possible to preserve affordable housing at scale while driving real community impact and economic growth.

A commitment now would show the country what bold leadership in housing truly looks like. It's the kind of move that proves when an institution truly lives its values, it doesn't just talk about bold change—it builds the future with it.

Like I've told the bank more than once, "You didn't just back the vision—you helped build it."

We pitched it to the federal government too. We needed them in the mix. I chased down then–Minister of Housing Sean Fraser so hard that I joked, "This guy's either going to meet with me or file a restraining order."

Eventually we met. When he landed in Halifax, we brought him straight to one of our properties at 30 Springhill so he could see the model in action. Meet the people. Feel the impact. Afterward we escorted him, Ron Lovett–security style, back to our office and laid it all out: "This isn't just about affordable housing. It's about healthcare, mental health, jobs, and community."

And he got it. He called VIDA's model an engine for economic growth for Canada. He also acknowledged that affordable housing is indeed a key part of Canadian infrastructure.

He's no longer in office, but the relationship stuck. We're still in talks with all levels of government and making progress. Working with government is a different game. That org chart is a moving target. One day you've got momentum. The next, your champions have moved to the Department of Justice.

We've said it before: government needs to be stubborn on vision and flexible on execution. Everyone agrees that we need more affordable housing. Few agree on the how. Even fewer are willing to try. So we did. And we've shown that a new model—one that treats residents like customers, builds trust, and delivers results—can work.

And people are noticing.

Eiryn Devereaux from the Nunavut Housing Corporation, who had been keeping a close eye on VIDA, reached out to me one day and said, "We need this in the North!"

So we invited him and his team to Halifax and showed them the model. By the end of the visit, they weren't asking *if*. They were asking *how*. And now we're in the process of bringing VIDA to Nunavut, not as owners or managers but by scaling what works: the training, the systems, the platform. We're helping them activate their own customers and build a model that's owned locally, led locally, and built for them, by them, with VIDA in their corner.

We've also welcomed BMO execs, Olympian Andre De Grasse, and leaders from across the country. Even the Trailer Park Boys. People are paying attention. Housing and affordability in general are on everyone's radar. They're curious how we are solving it, and they're watching what we do next.

So what's next?

We're now sitting across from some of the most influential people in the country, making the case to raise $300 million to preserve 7,000 affordable homes across Canada.

Not with big ideas, but with proof and a track record to back it up.

Proof that affordable housing can be preserved. That private capital can be part of the solution, not the problem. That our discipline could be just as bold as our ambition.

Every hard lesson. Every reinvention. Every time we could've walked away but chose to roll up our sleeves instead. It all led here.

We've shown it's possible to deliver affordable, sustainable solutions for Canadians and beyond, at scale and without compromise. And beneath all of that, something bigger was revealed:

What's possible when affordable housing is run by the right owner-operators.

So the next question isn't, *"Can it be done?"*

It's, *"Who's ready to join us to do more?"*

* * *

If you're a Canadian looking for an affordable place to call home — visit http://www.vidaliving.ca to apply.

If you're a housing operator — nonprofit, co-op, or government agency — looking for a financially viable way to run affordable housing, we've got a model worth seeing.

If you're an investor, family office, or philanthropist who believes in balancing purpose and profit — VIDA is proof that both can coexist.

If you manage institutional capital and seek real returns with real impact — we want to hear from you.

If you want to build world-class culture or decentralize without losing control — we've lived it, and we can help you do the same.

If you're part of any of the groups above and still a bit skeptical, come experience one of VIDA's communities and see the model — and real East Coast hospitality — in action. Email me at *ron@vidaliving.ca* to explore what's possible together.

PS: If you've read my books or follow my podcasts and you're here for the leadership and culture side of the story, don't worry. I'd never leave you hanging! There's a bonus chapter waiting for you.

Bonus Chapter

WHAT HOLDS IT ALL TOGETHER

WE DEBATED PUTTING THIS CHAPTER IN THE BOOK. After all, this isn't supposed to be a leadership or culture manifesto. But when we looked back at what actually held everything together through the chaos, the pressure, and the growth, one word kept coming up.

Culture.

Not the corporate "put it on a mug and call it a day" kind.

The kind that gets built day by day, mistake by mistake, through action, not words.

The kind that calls out the founder when he veers off course.

The kind that lets people go when they're not living the values, even if they're hitting targets, and helps them land new roles where they'll thrive.

The kind that shows up, digs in, and pushes through—together.

Yeah. That kind.

If you know me or you've been following our story, you already know I'm a fanatic about two things: decentralization and culture. I interview people about it. I read about it. Most importantly, I listen to our team. They teach me more about culture than any book or consultant ever could.

Culture is the heartbeat of everything we've built and the only way we've been able to scale without losing our edge.

So for all the culture junkies out there—the builders, the leaders, the HR rebels, the managers-turned-mentors, the ones who know that spreadsheets don't build great companies—this one's for you.

Because at VIDA, culture isn't the icing on the cake. It *is* the cake.

Let's dig in.

PART 1: CULTURE BY DESIGN
LESSON 1: YOU DON'T GET CULTURE BY ACCIDENT—YOU EARN IT BY DESIGN

When we hired our first chief operating officer, I could tell he got it right from the start.

He loved the culture. He dove deep into our values. You could see it in the way he listened, asked questions, paid attention. He didn't just like what we were doing. He believed in it. For him, it was like "Wow, this might be the first place that actually lives its values."

That was huge. But what really sold me on him came early on.

We were in our daily huddle, running through the usual. I made a comment about something we were planning to do. Nothing major. And right there, midmeeting, he stopped everything. "Hold on a second," he said. He had our values in front of him, and he started reading them back to me.

"You're saying this, but the values say that."

He wasn't just quoting them. He understood them. And

he was protecting them. He got the why behind every word. And he wasn't afraid to call out a mismatch between what we were saying and who we said we were.

Now let's be real: most people would never, and I mean never, call out the CEO in front of the entire team. But he did. He was calm, clear, and direct.

And honestly, it was music to my ears.

That was when I knew: finally someone else was watching the company's back.

Someone else was upholding the culture, not just following it.

Someone else was holding me to the exact same standard I expected from everyone else.

Right there on the spot, I told him, "You're absolutely right. We're changing course right now."

And I didn't just say it. I made sure the entire team saw it. This was culture in action. No hesitation. No soft landing. Just someone standing up for the standard. That's when you know it's real.

But we didn't get there overnight.

When we started VIDA, we weren't just launching a real estate company. We were rewriting the playbook on housing, community, and what it means to be a landlord. And we knew something that bold couldn't be built on borrowed values.

Lessons from the security company shaped that thinking. We saw what happened when values were vague. If they don't guide decisions, they're just noise. That's why, with VIDA, we got intentional from day one. We built a foundation around what mattered most: team-driven, relentless improvement and the courage to embrace change.

Values don't exist to make your website look good. They're a mirror. A gut check. A reminder of the nonnegotiables you stand for, especially when things get messy or it's time to course correct. They keep you accountable as a company. And if you're doing it right, you're designing them to hold the culture together.

That's why we treat values like systems. We revisit them, stress-test them, evolve them. Every challenge is a chance to future-proof the culture. So when something goes wrong, we ask, "What gap in our values let this happen, and how do we make sure this never cracks the culture again?"

So how do you know when it's time to evolve a value?

You pay attention to the real moments, especially that hard ones: when something breaks, when trust cracks, when a tough call puts your culture on the line. Those are your signals. That's when values either hold up or need to level up.

Like letting someone go. Not because they missed a deadline but because their attitude slowly wore down the team. Maybe the energy they brought in was consistently off—dismissive, draining, and contagious. One person like that is all it takes to start tipping the culture in the wrong direction.

That's when you say, "How do we make sure this doesn't happen again?" And your values get sharper.

Here's a great example: we were scaling fast, and suddenly we started hearing the same phrase pop up everywhere:

"I'm busy."

"Too busy."

"Sorry. I'm slammed."

It sounded normal. Everyone's busy, right?

But then we saw it for what it really was: a shield. A defence mechanism. A way to say, "Don't ask me for anything." And worse, it spread. One person said it, and their team picked it up. And before you knew it, "busy" became the reason no one helped each other.

We weren't having it.

So we flipped the script on busy and baked it into our values. We said, "Busy is good."

Busy means you're part of something growing. Busy means your work matters.

And we made it clear: if you're not up for being busy, this probably isn't your team.

And, yeah, we even had to let a few people go when they didn't want the pace. It wasn't about capability. It was about fit. And once we drew that line, we started celebrating it. "Busy" became something to be proud of, not an excuse to check out on your teammates.

That's how you keep culture honest and values alive: don't just talk about values. Pressure-test them. Because culture is not a set-it-and-forget-it thing. It's something you shape, refine, and rebuild over and over again.

And sometimes you take the basics for granted until life smacks you in the face with a reminder.

Like Kickback Kenny.

He was a great guy. Solid worker. Dependable. And then one day, we found out he'd been taking kickbacks from a supplier. You can't sweep that under the rug. He was representing our brand. Our name. Our values. There was only one option: we had to let him go.

It was a gut punch. No one wants to lose a good worker over a dumb decision. But this one was clear-cut.

Afterward, our team debriefed, and it hit us: we didn't have honesty and integrity written into our values.

The basics.

The foundation.

Missing!

Somewhere in our drive to build high-performing teams

and execute at scale, we skipped the part that said should have said, "Hey, just do the right thing."

There we were, humbled, a little embarrassed, but back at the drawing board. And we fixed it. Not by slapping *honesty* and *integrity* on a wall like every other company. It had to mean something. It had to feel real. So we brought it to the team—those who live the culture every day—and asked them to define it.

"At VIDA, we do the right thing even when no one's watching."

Simple. Real. Ours.

That's the balance. You can push for high performance, big results, speed, and innovation, but if you forget the basics like operating with integrity and honesty, it's like building a house on sand.

This lesson kicked off with a moment of real culture in action: someone calling out the CEO in front of the team and being right. That kind of moment doesn't happen by accident.

It happens by design.

It takes work to reach that level of alignment and shared ownership. And it doesn't start with policies or colourful words on a website. You choose values that are nonnegotiable. You bake them into how you hire, train, coach, and lead. You pay attention to the moments that test them. And when the pressure tests who you really are, you go back to the foundation and recalibrate. That's how culture stops being a concept and becomes a shared belief.

And if you want it to last, start where it begins: at the front door.

LESSON 2: YOU DON'T COACH VALUES – YOU HIRE THEM

At the security company, we introduced values during onboarding. Rookie mistake. By then, if the fit wasn't there, it was already a problem. So at VIDA, we flipped it: values come first. If someone doesn't align from the beginning, they don't move forward. Period.

But saying values matter is one thing. *Operationalizing* them is something else entirely. So we took it further. We asked ourselves, *What behaviours bring our values to life?*

Take innovation. Everyone wants it. But what trait really fuels it? Curiosity. And here at VIDA, curiosity isn't a bonus. It's the cost of entry. We're not here to tweak a broken housing system. We're here to reimagine the whole damn thing.

You don't get that from people who follow playbooks. You need people who ask sharper questions. Who push boundaries. Who come alive when there's no clear path, just possibility. You can't find that kind of fire on a CV.

That's why we leveraged AI to zero in on the behaviours that matter before someone even hits the interview stage. It strips away the fluff and shows us who's wired to think, question, and build from scratch. No resumés. No rehearsed answers. Just raw insight into who's got the mindset we need.

If you don't hit at least 85% on culture fit, you're not likely making it to round two. It's like airport security for your culture. You don't board the plane unless you clear the check. Skills get you in the line. Culture fit gets you through the gate.

No exceptions. No overhead baggage of ego allowed.

Because culture isn't something you protect on the back end. You filter for it on the front end.

And if it's a leadership role, that's a different game altogether.

LESSON 3: EARN THE TRUST BEFORE MAKING MOVES

Once the fit is locked, here comes the tricky part: our own version of the chicken or the egg. Do you hire someone because they fit the culture or because they can crush the role?

It's like choosing between pizza and fries. You want both. But sometimes you get stuck with a pizza that's all dough and no toppings. Or worse, pineapple on pizza when you're really *not* that person.

We've flip-flopped on this more than we'd like to admit. We've hired perfect culture fits—people we loved, people who brought the energy, people who just *got us*. We'd say, "Just get them in here. We'll figure out the job later!"

Sometimes, there *was no job* for them to figure out. We didn't have the right seat or they didn't have the skills. And other times we hired someone who was an absolute pro, brilliant at what they did, but they walked into our culture like a tuxedoed stranger at a pyjama party. We thought, *You're good at this job, but you're not one of us.*

We're now way more intentional, especially when it comes to leadership roles.

One senior leader went through eight or nine rounds of interviews. Why? Because we weren't just looking for a rock star. We needed someone who knew what band they were joining. It's like making sure your quarterback knows they're playing football, not cricket.

And when they came on board, we did something unusual.

We told them, "Don't touch anything for 90 days."

Ninety days of just watching. Listening. Observing. No playbook. No projects. Just soaking it all in. No direction.

It was like taking a kid into a candy store and saying, "Look, but don't touch." This can be torture for someone—especially someone hardwired to dive in and get stuff done.

By day 45, I could tell they were anxious. *They're going to think I'm not doing* anything, they probably thought. But we kept reassuring them, "You're doing exactly what you're supposed to. Be curious. Trust the process."

At the halfway point, we ran a check-in. Ten people sat around the table, firing off questions. "How would you describe our culture?" "What value feels off?" "Can you take us through your understanding of proactive maintenance?" "If you had to change one thing today, what would it be?"

Not quite an interrogation, but close.

And it worked.

We learned where they were comfortable and where they needed more time. That "don't touch anything" strategy wasn't a test. It was about syncing expectations and finding blind spots early. Letting the roots grow before expecting the plant to bloom.

It was a win for the company. We extended the 90-day runway beyond leadership and now use it for every hire. It gives people space to absorb the culture, earn trust, and see what really needs fixing before making any moves.

Hands down one of the smartest onboarding decisions we've ever made.

And it wasn't speed. It was patience—the kind that lets you listen.

LESSON 4: CULTURE HAS A PULSE – TAKE IT OFTEN

Building culture is one thing. Keeping it healthy takes a system.

You need a way to listen and respond in real time. That's why we turned our employee survey into something more than a check-the-box exercise. It's a diagnostic tool. A pulse check.

The VIDA Vibe Check, to be exact.

This isn't your typical "How's the last quarter been?" kind of thing. We ask the questions that matter: "Are we actually living our values?" "Do you see yourself working at VIDA in two years?"

And we go deep. "On a scale of 1 to 5, where 5 means leadership genuinely cares, how much do you feel they value your mental well-being?" We want the truth. No sugarcoating.

Every team gets its own data. Finance. Ops. Support. Building Services. No one-size-fits-all approach. Because each team lives a different reality. Finance isn't chasing down leaky pipes. Frontliners aren't dealing with spreadsheets.

Different pressures. Different rhythms. Different needs. Lumping them all together would be like giving one Yelp review for three different restaurants.

And when the results come in, we don't hide in a boardroom, nod solemnly, and file them under "Stuff We'll Get to Someday." We come together for the best part:

The debrief.

We start by celebrating the wins. Everyone loves a shout-out. But then we get into the hard stuff.

"How can we improve the 4 out of 5 score on mental health?"

This isn't a leadership show-and-tell. This is everyone at the table with their sleeves rolled up, fixing anything that's broken—together. Someone says, "Hey, my cousin's a therapist." Bam. That person is now leading the charge on our new mental wellness pilot.

The key is staying open about the challenges and giving your team the space to step up and solve them. That's real leadership. And it's change management 101.

Although we've built systems to design and maintain culture, structure and rhythm only take you so far. Because let's be real: culture isn't tested when things are working.

It's tested when something breaks or no longer fits. When it's time to part ways with something—or someone—that helped get you here. When you're so busy keeping up that you lose sight of what you're chasing.

And this is where Part II begins.

PART 2: HARD LESSONS ON LETTING GO
LESSON 5: YOU CAN'T CLING AND LEAD AT THE SAME TIME

I've faced a leadership challenge that's more common than most of us want to admit. I have been and continue to be a huge believer in the power of real-time feedback. Quick, honest, in-the-moment coaching, like a sports team. Spot the issue. Address it. Move forward.

But here's where I went wrong: as the relationships got deeper, I let them get in the way and started caring more about being *liked* than about being *helpful*. I avoided tough conversations. I softened the edges. I told myself, *They'll figure it out*.

But they didn't because I was clinging to comfort instead of offering clarity and saying what needed to be said. People don't need vague optimism. They need clarity. Direction. Truth. Ambiguity kills morale faster than failure ever could.

That's the trap: when you stay silent, people assume they're crushing it even when they're off track. And that's not leadership. That's neglect dressed up as kindness.

You need to sit down and say, "Here's where you're winning. Here's where you're stuck. And here's what needs to change."

It's easy to let this stuff slide. Business gets busy. Things move fast. Everyone's flying in different directions. You don't always notice when the job outgrows the original shape or when the mission demands something new.

You need to sit down and ask yourself, *Knowing what I know about the role today, would I be excited to rehire this person?* Because the longer you avoid the hard conversations, the heavier the cost.

We all cling sometimes. To roles. To people. To old ways of doing things. Why? Because they got us here. Because they felt safe. Because they *worked*.

But what got you here won't get you there. And clinging to the past is the fastest way to stall the future. I had to learn that sometimes the real act of leadership isn't holding on. It's having the guts to let go and the clarity to know when.

LESSON 6: LEADERSHIP MEANS HELPING PEOPLE LAND WHERE THEY BELONG

For me, loving your job comes down to three things:

You have to love the culture and the team.

You have to enjoy the work you do every day.

And you have to respect and connect with your leadership.

If even one of those is missing, things start to wobble. But when all three are solid, you get activated. You go all in.

Whenever something feels off, I always run it through that filter: *Is it a culture mismatch? A role that doesn't fit? A leadership disconnect?*

I've had my share of lessons when it comes to handling misalignment, especially after I've invested time and energy in someone.

You've been there, right? They've worked hard. Stayed late. Given you their blood, sweat, and tears. And, yeah, that counts for something. I believe in loyalty. That kind of commitment earns credit. You don't toss someone aside after a rough week.

But when there's a performance issue, especially when it's *not* cultural, you need to handle it with thought and care. Over the years, I've learned how to navigate these situations.

First step: honesty.

I sit down with them and have a real conversation. Not a performance review. A conversation. Do they see the misalignment too?

If they do and they're still open to coaching, I've got a starting point. From there, I ask, *Is there another seat on the bus where this person could actually thrive?* And I'm not talking about making up some half-baked role just to keep them around. I've made that mistake, and it doesn't help anyone. I'm talking about looking at what the company *actually* needs and asking whether their skillset, strengths, and energy fit better elsewhere.

For example, I've seen entrepreneurial-minded people struggle in finance. They hate the details, the precision, the repetition. But move them into sales or operations, and suddenly they're flying.

Same person. Different seat. Better fit.

Here's the key: it's not "Let's try this because you like the company" or "because you like me."

It has to be something they genuinely want.

So I give them time to reflect. We talk it through. I present a real path. And I make sure they understand exactly what success looks like in that new role. If they're in, we set a trial—usually six months. We both go in with open eyes and an understanding that if it's not working by the end of the trial, we'll part ways with respect.

And if that happens, we help them find a new role. We make the call. We support the next step.

Because sometimes it's just not a fit anymore, and that's

okay. But if there's no real opportunity, I don't pretend. I don't create a fake landing spot just to avoid a tough conversation.

That approach has been a game changer for me as a leader. It's helped us keep good people aligned, and it's helped people leave with their dignity and confidence intact.

The tricky part is that when more than one person doesn't fit, they tend to find each other. Misalignment attracts misalignment. They start bonding—not over solutions but over complaints. And that's a slippery slope where culture can start to erode. Fast.

We had that situation come up. You could see the stress written on his face. It wasn't just the workload. It was deeper. He came to me asking for more money. He was already being paid fairly. That's when you know it's probably not really about the money. It's *something else*.

And most of the time, that "something else" is that they're actually feeling undervalued, stuck, or just unhappy, and they think more money will solve it. Spoiler alert: it won't.

Now, I should add that my leadership style works great for the right kind of person. I'm high-energy, fast-moving, and direct. But for some people, it could feel like being thrown into the deep end with no life preserver. Without a doubt, I've probably triggered full-on panic in a few people over the years.

So as a leader, it's on me to recognize that. Some people thrive in my world. Others sink. And it's my responsibility to figure out which is which.

So I invited him to lunch. And I laid it out.

I said, "Look, I feel awful because I know *my* leadership is causing you stress. I can see it in your body language, your energy. It's weighing on you. And that's on me. Not you."

Then I gave him an out. I said, "Why don't we set you free? Let's help you find a place where you'll be happier. I'll open up my Rolodex. I'll help you land your next opportunity. I helped bring you here, and I'll help get you where you need to be next."

Those conversations are never easy. But honestly, they're often a bigger relief for the other person than they are for me. I've been in that seat, knowing deep down that something's off but too afraid to say it.

Sometimes the kindest thing you can do is just call it out. Name it. Release them. And let them walk into their next chapter with clarity and support.

Because leadership isn't about keeping everyone forever. It's about making sure they're in the right place, whether it's with you or without you.

LESSON 7: YOU DON'T SCALE BY HOLDING ON – YOU SCALE BY LETTING GO

Right around the time my first-born, Margot, arrived, I had one of the biggest leadership realizations of my life.

Focus isn't about trimming your to-do list. It's about protecting what matters most. For me that meant cutting the noise so the mission could stay front and centre.

I was juggling it all: running a roofing company, a culture consulting business, and a few other side ventures while staring down the Telus deal. A $100 million transaction bearing down like a freight train. I was all over the place. Classic shiny object syndrome. I knew if I didn't refocus right now, everything could fall apart.

VIDA was manageable back then. We had 300 units. But this deal was going to quadruple our size overnight. From 300 to 1,300 units. And to top it off, I had also committed to taking six months of paternity leave with Margot.

It was the perfect storm. But when the stakes go up, your priorities better get sharper. That was when I did something bold: I started saying no.

After two years of running Verne Harnish's advisory council, I stepped down. I left every local entrepreneur group I was part of. I walked away from three boards and wound down two side companies. I cut the noise and got laser-focused.

For an entrepreneur, saying no is brutal. We're wired to chase ideas. Stack that with my ADHD and dyslexia, and it's a full-blown circus with no ringmaster. And when everything's pulling at you, time isn't a luxury. It's the only edge you've got.

We were borrowing around $90 million for the Telus deal. My partners had $15 million of equity in the game. This wasn't just about money. It was about reputation. I wasn't going to be the guy who overextended and missed the mark. I was going to be the guy who delivered. That required discipline.

And I delivered by getting focused.

I cut all noise. I pulled the right people into the right seats. I drove the strategy forward, and then, come spring, I stepped back. I took five full months off to be with Margot. I only touched what was absolutely necessary. Everything else I let go.

And I don't regret a second of it.

People say, "You can't take time off when you're in the middle of something big." That's nonsense. I was in the middle of the biggest deal of my career—a deal that mattered to me, my team, our partners, and Atlantic Canada. And I still stepped away.

Not because I'm superhuman.

But because when you build real culture—trust, ownership, shared purpose—*you can* get out of the way. *You should* get out of the way. The team runs with it. They lead. They deliver.

Before I left, I had an important conversation with the

leadership team. I said, "When I come back, I don't want to be the same leader I was before. I want to know where I should lean in and where I need to let go."

The feedback was gold.

"Stay focused on strategy. People and culture. But the details? Get out of the weeds."

So when I came back, I did exactly that. I stayed out of the weeds. I stayed in my lane. And everything got faster, smoother, and stronger. That time with Margot changed me. That focus changed VIDA. And that one conversation with the team changed the way I lead forever.

* * *

These days, my leadership is all about mastering communication, but not just saying the right things. Anyone can do that. That's not the game.

I'm talking about becoming the kind of communicator who fuels connection. A leader who brings out the best in *anyone*, no matter their background, personality, or learning style. That's the real challenge. And truthfully, it's not always smooth sailing.

Because when it comes to mastering the art of communication, I've learned this:

Words are the smallest part of the equation.

It's the tone. The energy. The body language. That's where connection lives.

When you get *that* part right, the words almost don't matter. People don't just hear you. They *feel* you. Because at the end of the day, culture *is* communication. It's how trust gets built. How energy spreads. How the whole damn thing holds, especially when the pressure hits.

Try scaling a business without it. It'll snap under pressure. Every time.

At VIDA, culture isn't the soft stuff. It's the infrastructure. The operating code that makes everything else possible—growth, strategy, execution. And I hear it all the time: "Culture eats strategy for breakfast." And I'm all in on that. But here's my upgrade: if that's true, if culture really is more powerful than strategy, then you'd better be strategic about your culture.

Culture hires the team, drives the bus, picks the destination, and tells you when to hit the brakes. And if you're not designing for that, if you're not fighting for it, shaping it, pressure-testing it, no amount of vision will get you there.

I'd put our culture up against anyone's.

World class. No question.

Because at VIDA, culture doesn't just eat strategy for breakfast. It sits at the head of the damn table.

Acknowledgments

BUILDING VIDA HAS BEEN ONE OF THE MOST MEANING-ful journeys of my life, built on purpose, resilience, and a deep belief in the power of community. When I sold my security company in 2017, I walked away with a lesson that changed everything: true success isn't just about scaling a business. It's about building something rooted in culture, collaboration, and decentralization—something that actually makes people's lives better.

As VIDA took shape, so did the scale of the housing crisis across Canada. Tackling that crisis has been anything but easy. But every inch of progress we've made has been because of the remarkable people who have shown up, stood beside us, and poured their hearts into this mission.

To our entire VIDA community—the Support Centre, Building Ambassadors, Team Captains, Building Services, and Community Contractors: thank you. Your passion, grit, and dedication transform everyday buildings into vibrant communities. You are the soul of VIDA, and everything we've built stands on your shoulders.

To our legal and professional advisors—BMO, Deloitte, McInnes Cooper—and the many others who've lent us their time and wisdom: your guidance has helped us build not just fast but strong. Your insights have been critical to building something that will stand the test of time.

To our investors, partners, and suppliers: thank you for believing in a vision that blends purpose with performance. Your support makes that possible. To the members of our HR Advisory Council and the Canadian NOAH Preservation Fund advisory committee: thank you for helping shape the long game. Your wisdom is in the DNA of this company.

To the customers who call VIDA home: thank you for your patience, feedback, ideas, and trust. You've challenged us to get better every day. You've helped us shape a new model for housing. You are not just tenants. You are our teachers, and we are endlessly grateful.

To the team behind this book—Lisa Caskey, Rachael Williams, and Joel Goodman: thank you for helping capture the heartbeat of this journey. And to Jaclyn Saunders, unofficial editor-in-chief and strategic gut check behind every page: this book has your fingerprints all over it!

To my friends and family: thank you for standing by me through the late nights, the early mornings, and the relentless pursuit of something bigger than myself. To my wife, Natalie: you are my rock, my compass, and my constant. Thank you for being all in. To Georgia, Wellington, and Margot: you are my reason, my why. I hope you grow up knowing that anything is possible when you lead with purpose and back it with courage.

And finally, to the underdogs—the overlooked, the underestimated, the ones trying to do something meaningful in a world that doesn't always make it easy: this book is for you.

If you've ever been told you're dreaming too big, aiming too high, or moving too fast, don't stop.

Keep building. Keep pushing. Keep proving them wrong.

The world needs what you have to offer.

About the Author

RON LOVETT is the founder and CEO of VIDA, an entrepreneur, a globally recognized author, a speaker, and a business thought leader. He previously transformed the physical security industry by founding Source Security, scaling the company to over 3,500 staff before exiting at a 24x multiple. Known for his renegade spirit, Ron builds high-performing, decentralized organizations with world-class cultures where everyone is a passionate stakeholder. A five-time recipient of the *Atlantic Business Magazine* Top 50 CEO award, Ron serves on boards and supports organizations like the Fraser Institute, Shift Canada, the ROM, and Futurpreneur Canada. He lives with his wife and three children in Halifax, Nova Scotia, where he mentors young entrepreneurs.

www.ingramcontent.com/pod-product-compliance
Lightning Source LLC
Chambersburg PA
CBHW030516210326
41597CB00013B/928